Many times when we hear the term "new covenant," we nod and shake our heads without really understanding the meaning of "covenant." And so we easily waiver in our identity and acceptance before God. This book will help you grasp God's fierce and unwavering commitment to His children as you explore the depths of covenant.

—Jodi Seidler
Director of International Growth
Elim Fellowship

In order to reap the rich blessings of grace-filled relationships, every Christian needs a basic understanding of covenant. In *Drinking Truth*, Bob Santos has served for us a rich libation full of the fundamental covenantal elements of our faith. I wholeheartedly encourage every believer to imbibe in this insightful and enjoyable offering of *Drinking Truth*.

—Pastor Bob Dunsmore
Lead Pastor
Covenant Way Church

Many Christians live in ignorance of the covenant foundations of the Christian faith and their significance to our daily lives. In *Drinking Truth*, Bob Santos clearly lays out both a historical background of Biblical covenants and their relevance to the current culture in which we are living. He creatively draws parallels to help readers embrace truths that will strengthen their faith and understanding of what they believe and why they believe it. This is an excellent tool to help build a strong foundation that will last.

—John Cavari
Lead Pastor
Garner Christian Fellowship

The church today has lost some of the most important promises and concepts in God's Word. One of those concepts is the teaching on covenants. From Genesis to Malachi, the Lord lays out a foundation of promises that are tied to the covenants. This book will expand your understanding of who you are in Christ and how to live in the fullness of the covenant of grace today. I recommend the incredibly rich teaching on the covenants that you will find within the pages of this book, so dig in and enjoy the banquet that Bob has prepared for you.

—Paul Edwards
Retired Professor of Theology
Elim Bible Institute and College

Drinking Truth is an insightful look into the depths of God's love for humanity. By bringing every major covenant in the Bible together in one concise book, Bob not only teaches, but also inspires a closer walk with God.

—Pastor Todd Pugh
Lead Pastor
Kiski Valley Community Church

Bob Santos has given us an important reminder that our God is a covenant-making and covenant-keeping God. We would do well to understand this oft-overlooked aspect of God's character, for it will relieve us of a works mentality. In the process, we will be reminded that we can accept or reject His covenant, but we cannot alter it. Thank you, Bob, for this relevant and well-written reminder that we approach God not based on our own merits, but on the basis of His shed blood that established the new covenant in Christ.

—Dr. John Stanko
President
PurposeQuest International

DRINKING TRUTH

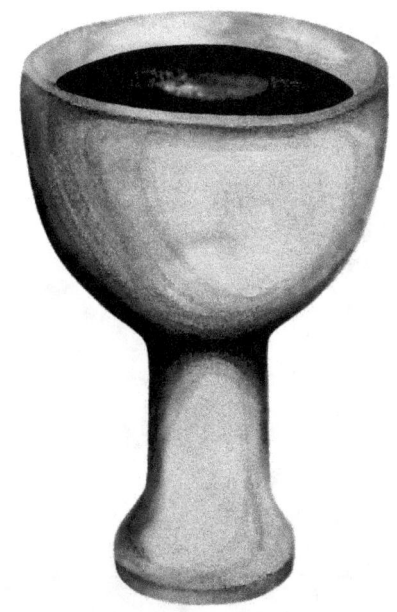

Embracing the Covenant
Mindset of the Bible

DRINKING TRUTH

Embracing the Covenant Mindset of the Bible

BOB SANTOS

Search for Me Ministries, Inc.
Indiana, PA

Drinking Truth: Embracing the Covenant Mindset of the Bible
By Bob Santos

Copyright © 2019 by Search for Me Ministries, Inc.

Cover Design: Gaffney Printables
Cover Photo: Steve Margita
Interior Artwork: Katie Stevens
Editor: Crystal Min (http://www.crystalclearenglish.com)

Unless otherwise noted, all Scripture quotations are taken from the New American Standard Bible® (NASB), Copyright © 1960, 1962, 1963, 1968, 1971, 1972, 1973, 1975, 1977, 1995 by The Lockman Foundation. Used by permission. www.Lockman.org

Scripture quotations marked (ESV) are from the ESV® Bible (The Holy Bible, English Standard Version®). ESV® Text Edition: 2016. Copyright © 2001 by Crossway, a publishing ministry of Good News Publishers. The ESV® text has been reproduced in cooperation with and by permission of Good News Publishers. Unauthorized reproduction of this publication is prohibited. All rights reserved.

Scripture quotations marked (NLT) are taken from the *Holy Bible*, New Living Translation, Copyright © 1996, 2004, 2007, 2013, 2015 by Tyndale House Foundation. Used by permission of Tyndale House Publishers, Inc., Carol Stream, Illinois 60188. All rights reserved.

Scripture quotations marked (NKJV) are taken from the New King James Version®. Copyright © 1982 by Thomas Nelson. Used by permission. All rights reserved.

Published by SfMe Media
Indiana, PA 15701
www.sfme.org

Printed in the United States of America

Library of Congress Control Number: 2019953015

ISBN: 978-1-937956-22-6
ePub ISBN: 978-1-937956-23-3

Dedicated to my family. By God's grace, blessings I once struggled to imagine have become my present reality.

Contents

Introduction		11
Part I: Covenant Basics		**17**
1.	More than an Agreement	19
2.	The Heart of God's Covenants	35
Part II: Early Covenants of the Bible		**53**
3.	The Cursed Planet	55
4.	Abraham's Legacy of Faith	73
5.	The Mosaic and Davidic Covenants	89
Part III: The Marriage Covenant		**105**
6.	The Covenant Family	107
7.	Outside the Lines	125
Part IV: The New Covenant		**143**
8.	The New Covenant in Blood	145
9.	Our Forever Mediator	163
10.	Bound by Love	179
11.	The Prevailing Church	197
12.	Living Out the New Covenant	215
About the Author		233
Acknowledgments		235
Additional Resources		237

INTRODUCTION

The more I understand of our Creator's ways, the more I find myself both awed by His goodness and mortified by our ignorance. The purpose of this book is to dispel some of that ignorance so that we might more fully embrace the goodness of God. To better communicate my perspective, I will begin with a personal story.

In the early days of our marriage, my wife Debi maintained our lawn. So, I was more than happy to oblige when she asked for a trimmer—as in a weed-eater—one year for Mother's Day. (A wise husband will not follow this example indiscriminately.) The tool worked well but had one major drawback: the need to stay connected to an electrical outlet. What a pain it was to drag a long extension cord around the yard just to knock down a few weeds! Perhaps that is why the upkeep of our yard soon became my responsibility.

I felt no grief the day that trimmer severed its last weed. Sensing an opportunity for yard care liberty, I purchased one of the early lithium battery models. I cannot say that it made lawn care fun, but I relished the improvement nonetheless.

Over time, my two 20 volt (V) batteries began to lose their strength, leaving me with a bit of a dilemma. I did not want to discard a still-working trimmer, but the batteries were expensive, and the machine had weathered quite a few seasons. My decision was made when I came across a 40 V trimmer-blower combination set in a local home improvement store. Still reluctant to send the old weed-eater to the landfill, I put it in the corner of our garage.

The new trimmer worked great for several weeks. Unfortunately for me, everything changed one Saturday when I decided to help out a neighbor next to our ministry center who was having difficulty finding someone to mow his grass.

The morning had been going well, but when I decided to switch the battery from the blower to the trimmer, my downward yard care spiral began. Suddenly, the battery was tight and would not fully slide into the trimmer's connection. The plastic housing seemed to have shifted. The farther I pushed the battery into the housing, the harder it became to get it out again. Soon it was stuck, and I could not move it in or out.

By this time, I was fuming. Saturdays provide a rare opportunity for me to catch up on my work around the house, and because of that "piece of junk," I had barely started on my project list. Irritated and determined, I drove home to find the receipt so I could return the machine to the store. In another unfortunate turn of events (for me), Debi was spending the day with a friend, and finding the receipt without her help proved to be an elusive task. After taking about thirty minutes to locate and sort through a pile of paperwork, I found it at last. Even more irritated, I climbed back into my SUV and set a course for the other side of town.

Upon arriving at the home improvement store, I decided to try sliding the battery out one last time. As I tugged with all my might, that heavy 40 V battery suddenly let loose and popped into the air, hitting me squarely in the mouth. Wincing from the pain, I reached to catch the thing with my hand, and then with my foot, as it bounced around. After failing on both attempts, I watched helplessly as the once-new battery rolled along the hard asphalt parking lot. I snatched it up and breathed a sigh of relief when a close examination revealed only a few minor scratches and no cracks. Then, reaching up to touch my bruised lip, I felt something wet. Yep, that was blood smeared on my finger. Now I was really mad!

Marching into the store, I went straight to the customer service desk to return the defective trimmer. My day did not improve from there. The teenage worker asked when I had purchased it, and then politely informed me that the thirty-day return period had expired.

INTRODUCTION

I could contact the manufacturer, but the store would not help me. At that moment, I wanted to scream in that youngster's face and call down divine judgment from heaven, but I knew she was just doing her job. Setting policies was beyond her pay grade, and a customer's tirade would only make her day as bad as mine. Biting my already bleeding lip, I took my defective trimmer and moped out the door.

Back at home, I sat down on the front porch steps with a file and rubber mallet. I was determined to fix the problem, but no amount of effort, including a few taps with the mallet, could establish the connection to the trimmer. So there I sat, frustrated and fuming about defective products and lousy customer service policies.

As I stared at my Saturday morning folly, a realization began to dawn. The connection between the battery and the trimmer seemed odd—as though they were of a different design. Comparing the trimmer to the blower, I found myself befuddled by the difference. "Why in the world would a company make those differently?" I asked myself.

At that moment, I had what you might call a "home improvement epiphany." Walking back into the garage, I looked at the tool rack to see my shiny new trimmer sitting where I had left it the week prior. Nothing was defective; I had been trying to fit the new 40 V battery onto my *old* 20 V trimmer! I have probably done dumber things in my life, but not many.

Based on its title, it is evident that this book has nothing to do with lawn care, or defective tools, or customer service return policies. The story of my stupidity, however, provides an excellent, albeit embarrassing, illustration to introduce the topic of *covenant*.

God's interaction with humanity has always been defined by covenant relationships—or the lack thereof—but rarely does the Western church operate with a covenantal mindset. And so it is that many Christian teachings make little or no sense to us. Feeling confused, offended, and even a bit smug, some people malign the Bible—and its God—because it fails to conform to our Western sense of propriety. Others want to believe, while struggling to reconcile what they read in the Bible with the God they envision. But just as there was no inherent problem with my supposedly defective trimmer, or even the home improvement store's return policy, so also there is nothing "wrong" with the teachings of the Scriptures and the God who inspired them. What we fail to recognize is that the problem is ours. It is our blind ignorance that leaves us wanting, but in typical human fashion, we are prone to cast blame anywhere but in our own direction.

Drinking Truth: Embracing the Covenant Mindset of the Bible is my effort to explain why God's plan for humanity is magnificent in every way. If you are unfamiliar with the concept of covenant, the Christian faith should make far more sense by the time you turn the final page of this book.

One claim I do not make, however, is that *Drinking Truth* will be an easy read. In addition to a contrary way of thinking, those in the Western world face at least three mountainous obstacles. First, recent changes in our cultural perspectives of sexual relationships have taken us further from God's design. Second, those who have experienced the pain of a failed marriage often prefer to avoid the topic of covenant altogether. Finally, many of us have been born into families that are far from ideal. Simply thinking about the issue can evoke painful memories.

My goal is always to educate and encourage, but I find it nearly impossible to avoid that uncomfortable feeling one gets when confronted by the hard truth that God's ways differ vastly from ours. Some of our ignorance regarding such an important topic is intentional because truth can be an uncomfortable ally. For while the Lord's "cup of truth" overflows with spiritual vigor, it sometimes tastes bitter going down. *Everyone wants the liberty that the cup of truth brings, but few want to consume its contents.*

God's reality is more than worthy of any angst we might feel as His light exposes our shortcomings. The Lord's truth is the cure for what ails us. In it, we find life, hope, wholeness, freedom, and transformation. Yes, truth might at times go down like medicine, but without it we are spiritually sick, captives of lofty thoughts that promise life and freedom but deliver only cheap substitutes. If we can learn to get "comfortable" with the discomfort that truth brings, we will position ourselves to experience the greater substance of God's reality.

Without a firm grasp of the Bible's covenantal perspective, our lives will forever risk falling short of the depth and potential of the good Lord's plans. Furthermore, those who profess the name of Christ will be ill-prepared to handle extreme adversity, including the physical persecution now afflicting so many of our Christian brothers and sisters across the globe. Our world is being shaken, and institutions we once revered as trustworthy no longer hold our confidence. One painful consequence is that we are becoming an increasingly anxious society.

Have you ever considered that the shaking is intentional, that in these days our Creator seeks to redirect our trust to that which can never be shaken? God's ways might be mysterious to us, but they are never wrong. And the more that we grasp the reality of a covenantal mindset, the more we realize that there has never been—and never will be—any fault in the God who created us.

As much as it might slight a person's ego to admit, our thoughts are *not* the standard for truth. There is so much that we do not know, and what we think we know is not always accurate. I *thought* that a defective trimmer was my problem, but my own shortsightedness was really to blame. *If we honestly want to know truth, we must take time to listen, turn off the automatic responses in our minds, and seek to understand.*

The covenantal mindset of the Bible might differ radically from what we are accustomed to, but embracing this perspective will enable us to know the depths of His faithfulness in ways that Western culture never can. In the end, we will see that there is much more to the faithfulness of God than any of us have yet imagined.

PART I
COVENANT BASICS

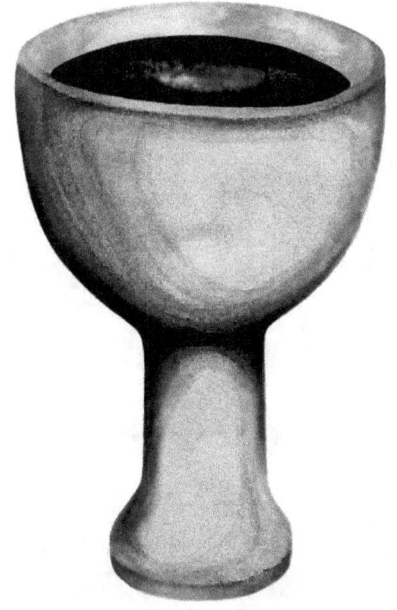

Your lovingkindness, O Lord, extends to the heavens,
Your faithfulness reaches to the skies.
Psalm 36:5

CHAPTER ONE

MORE THAN AN AGREEMENT

*"My covenant I will not violate,
Nor will I alter the utterance of My lips."*

Psalm 89:34

"If you mean what you say, you will drink truth with me."

—The old Gecho chief

Before pastoring the Cranston St. Baptist Church in Providence, Rhode Island, Rev. Moses H. Bixby served as a missionary in the Southeast Asian nation of Burma—now frequently referred to as Myanmar. One might expect that a nineteenth-century Westerner working with primitive people such as the wild Karens might have a few stories to tell, and that was certainly the case with Bixby. The vast differences in culture, as evidenced in his account of a conversation with a Karen tribal chief, exposes us to a mentality that has been all but lost to the Western world:

> "If you mean what you say," said the old chief of the Gecho tribe to me, referring to my professions of friendship, "you will drink truth with me." "Well, what is drinking truth?" I said. In reply, he said: "This is our custom. Each chief pierces his arm—draws blood—mingles it in a vessel with whisky

[sic], and drinks of it; both promising to be true and faithful to each other, down to the seventh generation."[1]

According to the old chief, "drinking truth" meant entering into a sacred covenant relationship, which then established a level of trust that the modern West can only envy. When a blood bond was made, either party could trust the other to be true and faithful regardless of the cost. Everyone understood that a covenant-friend could be called upon, even at the risk of his own life, in times of deepest need.

To our modern, "civilized" minds, the idea of a blood-covenant ceremony seems both bizarre and grotesque—a practice best reserved for the realms of book and movie fantasy. There was a time, however, when practically every culture had what we might call a "covenantal worldview." It was an era when people's mindsets were defined by their covenant relationships.

Over time, Western culture drifted away from a covenantal mentality, creating a huge disconnect between truth and trust. What, for example, comes to mind when discussing the dealings of early European immigrants and the U.S. government with Native Americans? Broken treaties. Yes, each opposing party shared fault throughout those early conflicts, but differing mindsets exacerbated the issues. Many early Native Americans lived with a covenantal worldview, and so they were mystified—even incensed—when the U.S. government seemed to create its own "truth" by breaking treaties that it had forged with solemn oaths. Since that time, many vestiges of covenantal thinking in the West have faded into cultural legend.

An interesting example of a covenant can be found in a 2009 case, where Texas financier Allen Stanford was sentenced to 110 years in prison after being convicted of defrauding investors through a seven-billion-dollar Ponzi scheme.[2] Media accounts reported that

---

1. H. Clay Trumbull, *The Blood Covenant* (Kirkwood, MO: Impact Books, 1975), 316.
2. Antonié Warwick-Young Walsh and Albert D. Spalding Jr., "Recognizing and Responding to Red Flags: The *Stanford* Ponzi Scheme," *Journal of Legal Issues and Cases in Business*, accessed October 22, 2019, https://www.aabri.com/manuscripts/11829.pdf.

Stanford was able to prolong his deception because he had made a "blood oath" with the director (Leroy King) of Antigua's Financial Services Regulatory Commission.

One of Stanford's associates reported that Leroy King and Stanford had cut their wrists and mingled their blood as part of a "brotherhood" ceremony. As a result of this *blood covenant*, King was bound to secrecy and sworn to prevent Stanford's illegal business dealings from being discovered. Thus, according to the reports, the regulatory commission that had been entrusted with the task of overseeing Stanford's bank not only turned a blind eye, but also helped perpetuate the cover-up.

Seven billion dollars is a profound amount of money, and I cannot imagine the pain that this situation caused to the investors who lost their savings. At the same time, the tone of the story got me thinking. The story of people honoring a blood oath was treated as a bizarre rite by the media outlets covering the case. What was once considered a normal cultural practice is now something that shocks us because of its peculiarity.

About a decade after Stanford's sentencing, reports began to surface about the breakup of celebrities Brandon Jenner and his wife Leah after six years of marriage and one child:

> "Hi everybody, it is with love in our hearts that we feel it's time to share some personal news with you all. After celebrating fourteen beautiful years together, we have lovingly come to the decision to end the romantic aspect of our relationship," they said. "We are deeply proud of the life we've cultivated together and are truly grateful for the bond of friendship we hold and cherish today. It is stronger than ever."
>
> "Even though we have chosen to separate as a couple, we still love one another very, very much and remain a major part of each other's lives—as best friends, family and loving parents to our daughter," they continued. "There has been no lying or cheating or fighting that prompted this change, just an

expansion of our individual evolution which has inspired us to support each other in a new way. We are still, very much, a loving family and are bonded by a deep connection that is rooted in love."[3]

While Stanford's story of a blood covenant being honored was considered peculiar, the reaction to this divorce announcement was treated as relatively normal. There may have been a touch of sadness in a few accounts, but reporters mentioned nothing about violating a sacred marriage covenant.

These stories—and many others—typify our modern societal mindsets. Once-normal behavior is now considered bizarre, and actions previously viewed as scandalous are now treated with a sense of normalcy. My purpose is not to judge; I just want to understand. Situations like these make me question whether such changes are a matter of cultural progress—of moving on from the "dark ages" of small-minded and restrictive thinking—or whether Western culture has lost an essential element of human meaning.

DANGEROUS TERRITORY

Though you might not be familiar with the name Alexander Pope, you probably have heard a few of this eighteenth-century poet's sayings such as, "To err is human, to forgive divine," and "Fools rush in where angels fear to tread." Pope also coined the phrase, "A little learning is a dangerous thing."

> A little learning is a dangerous thing;
> Drink deep, or taste not the Pierian spring:
> There shallow draughts intoxicate the brain,
> And drinking largely sobers us again.[4]

---

3. Aurelie Corinthios, "Brandon Jenner and Leah Jenner Split After 14 Years," PEOPLE.com, September 10, 2018, accessed October 22, 2019, https://people.com/tv/brandon-jenner-leah-jenner-split/.
4. Alexander Pope, "An Essay on Criticism: Part 2," Poetry Foundation, accessed October 22, 2019, https://www.poetryfoundation.org/poems/44897/an-essay-on-criticism-part-2.

Pope was referring to the mythical "Pierian spring"—the supposed source of knowledge for the arts and sciences. While we might find a small drink of knowledge exhilarating, it is also dangerous. To grasp the full depth of knowledge, we must drink deeply. As we do, our eyes are opened to see beyond our limited understanding.

The idea that "a little learning is a dangerous thing" applies to the Bible as much as anything. Throughout the centuries, we have seen legalistic mindsets, cultic rituals, and even false prophets arise among well-intentioned souls who misunderstood key principles of Scripture. This tendency toward error persists even in our day, and nowhere is it truer than with the covenantal mindset in which the Bible was penned.

As an example, many modern teachers have seized upon the reality that "God is love" (1 John 4:8), only to apply that truth according to our current cultural thinking. The dangerous result is a "love is God" mentality. Thus, anything done in the name of love must, without question, be birthed of God. With feelings of love as our justification, we are free to do just about anything guilt-free— or so we might think. From a Biblical perspective, however, love and faithfulness go hand in hand. More specifically, those who live by God's *law of love* embrace the necessity of sacrificial living. It is for very good reason that the apostle Paul prayed that the love of the Philippian church would abound with "real knowledge and all discernment" (Philippians 1:9).

Sadly, it seems as though gangs and organized crime groups have a better understanding of covenantal faithfulness than do many of us in the church. Criminal enterprises, these days, place far more weight on the concepts of sacrificial living and brotherhood than do many who profess to follow Christ. And though I have seen increased Christian teaching on the topic of covenant in recent years, more progress is needed in communicating this necessary concept.

The thought that the Western church lacks a core element of understanding might seem incredulous to some. I mean, we now have more access to Bible-based teaching resources than any other culture in the history of our world. How can we be largely ignorant of such an important concept? Part of the problem lies in the fact that the Bible does not provide a clear explanation of the meaning and significance of covenants. In that era, the principles involved were common knowledge. As a result, there was no reason for the ancients to explain something that everybody already knew.

Well-meaning efforts to make the Christian faith culturally relevant have compounded our struggle. And while I champion the value of meeting people where they are, I also know that the wise and holy Creator of our vast cosmos will never adjust His mindset to our earthly thinking. Cultural relevance, therefore, should be but a *starting point*. Do we truly want to know the Lord and experience His blessings to the fullest? Such goals cannot be achieved unless we strive for a deeper understanding of His ways and align our lives accordingly. Teachers, specifically, are given the solemn responsibility to communicate His truths without compromising their integrity.

Unless we make a concerted effort to understand and convey the covenantal mindset of the Bible, we will view many of God's actions as cruel or bizarre. We will also risk seeing Western Christianity spiral down in flaming defeat. *Cultural relevance can never carry people through times of dark adversity and persecution; our strength must be drawn from the deeper truths that make for substantive faith.*

Blood oaths and sacred pacts do more than make for interesting reading; they point us toward a more accurate understanding of God upon which we can establish a rock-solid faith. From start to finish, the Bible was written through the lens of a covenantal worldview. But if our modern mindsets are out of sync with the writers of Scripture, drinking deeply of God's truth becomes something like trying to suck jello through a thin straw. Those seeking to imbibe of the soul-satisfying truths of the Scriptures are compelled to pursue an accurate understanding of what its writers sought to communicate. Without comprehending the mindset through which their life-giving words were inked, we are left to fill in the cultural void with mentalities of a different era.

WHAT IS A COVENANT?

From a Biblical perspective, *a covenant is a sacred and binding relationship of the highest order—a solemn pact or treaty.* A covenant is more than just an agreement and different from a contract. A contract is written in an effort to protect one's personal interests, often being subject to change or negotiation. Covenants, in contrast, are *unchangeable* and established with a willingness to make extreme sacrifices for the sake of another person or group.

According to the late Dr. Meredith G. Kline, an Old Testament scholar and expert in covenant theology:

> The berith [the Hebrew word translated as "covenant"] arrangement is no mere secular contract but rather belongs to the sacred sphere of divine witness and enforcement.[5]

Kline's observation shouts to the heavens! Modern contracts might require legal commitment, but they lack the element of sacred devotion. When the witness of God is drawn into a covenant relationship, trust and faithfulness to the covenant skyrocket in importance. Without such an understanding, we are inclined to treat a sacred trust flippantly.

In the world of professional sports, for example, it is not uncommon for a star athlete to refuse to play in the final year of a contract (which all parties had willingly signed) in an attempt to negotiate a better deal. A press release by the superstar might say, "This is a business, and I need to do what's best for me and my family." Such a mindset might characterize contemporary thought, but it strays far from a covenantal mindset.

One of the better present-day examples of a covenantal mentality might involve the members of a military unit. Their bonds are so strong that they develop a "no man left behind" mindset that is lived out even at great personal risk. Covenants in the ancient sense,

---

5. Meredith G. Kline, *Kingdom Prologue: Genesis Foundations for a Covenantal Worldview,* (Eugene, OR: Wipf and Stock Publishers, 2006), 1.

however, were also innately spiritual. Oaths were not simply made; they were proclaimed as sacred expressions of devotion to religious deities. The "so help me God" phraseology of a modern court oath, for example, has roots that reach far back into history.

If any group of people *should* grasp the depths of covenant faithfulness, it would be the genuine followers of Jesus Christ. Sadly, such is not always the case. Recently, I read a Christian book as part of a study course. The work was done well, but one thing made the hair on my neck bristle. The author used the words "covenant," "agreement," and "contract" interchangeably. The fact that a seasoned Christian leader would interchange these words exemplifies the ignorance of our Western version of the Christian faith.

Covenants are marked by awesome blessings when they are honored and terrible curses when broken. But when members of a church missions team, for example, are asked to sign a "covenant" regarding their behavior on a trip, there is no force to the agreement. No one is happy if a team member fails to honor the terms, but severe consequences are rare. Failure to keep a real covenant, on the other hand, would result in an extreme curse-infused penalty—such as being dragged for several miles behind a fifteen-passenger church van. Clearly, the mindsets that characterize the vast majority of our church agreements stray far from the "drinking truth" mentality of ancient covenant bonds. Such misuse of the concept is dangerous in that it renders as common a concept that is innately sacred.

The Hebrew word *berith* is often used in the Old Testament when speaking of a covenant.[6] The New Testament's Greek language employed the word *diathēkē*, which can also be translated as our English "testament."[7] The word testament itself is of Latin origin and can mean either a covenant or a last will and testament. If we think of *diathēkē* in the sense of a solemn declaration of one's will, we can see how the word might apply to either situation.

---

6. Robert L. Thomas, *New American Standard Hebrew-Aramaic and Greek Dictionaries: Updated Edition* (Anaheim: Foundation Publications, Inc., 1998).
7. Thomas, *New American Standard Hebrew-Aramaic and Greek Dictionaries: Updated Edition.*

Sadly, the evolution of language has left us with an unhealthy impression. What would be more aptly titled, *The Old Covenant* and *The New Covenant,* are now labeled, *The Old Testament* and *The New Testament.* Rather than viewing the New Testament as a collection of sacred writings that proclaim the blessings of a devoted relationship with God, people tend to see it either as a record of events or a list of instructions left by Jesus for us to follow. The relational element has been lost to many—and with tragic results. This disappointing development provides yet another reminder of the loss of covenantal thinking, saddling many churches with a rule-based (legalistic) mindset that runs contrary to Christ's gospel of grace.

Through the many small group Bible studies I have led, I have encountered far too many people whose childhood religious experiences were replete with heavy-handed requirements to meet unattainable standards. Sadly, these genuine souls were forced to endure an abundance of needless pain. Even worse, many of their contemporaries chose to abandon the Christian faith. I will address the issue of legalism more thoroughly in the future, but we must first lay a necessary foundation by proclaiming that *the Bible is first and foremost a book of relationship.*[8] In it, we find not merely instructions to follow, but also the wisdom to walk with God and align our lives with His design. Those who see the Bible as "God's Rule Book" need to take a step back and reevaluate their understanding of the gospel.

TREATIES

Treaties are generally rooted in covenantal thinking, and in Old Testament times, there were two basic types. One was called a "suzerain" treaty and the other a "parity." A quick look at each type will help further our understanding of covenantal thought.

In a suzerain treaty, a dominant country (suzerain) established a covenant with a weaker nation to make it a subordinate (vassal) state. Usually, these treaties provided elements of protection for the weaker

---

8. *The TouchPoint: Connecting with God through the Bible* provides an introduction to the Bible with a relational emphasis.

entity, but for the most part, the dominant state established terms that were favorable to itself.

A parity treaty involved a covenant between two essentially equal parties. In many cases, these pacts were highly personal and emphasized *relational oneness*. Two individuals or groups became one in spirit and heart. This type of covenant provides us with a powerful, albeit imperfect, image of the relationship between the Father, Son, and Holy Spirit.

The majority of the covenants between God and humanity seem to be a combination of the two types of treaties. They are suzerain in the sense that God sets the terms; however, His terms are far more relational and favorable than those found in man-made suzerain treaties. In either case, the ancient concept identified by the Hebrew word *berith* "was heavy in the sense of commitment to an obligation," according to Kline.[9] Both parties were expected to regard the keeping of a covenant with the utmost sanctity.

The establishment of a covenant usually involved a ceremony, which had the potential to create logistical problems when large groups of people were involved. For practical purposes, a *covenant representative* would act on behalf of each group. Those who did not participate in the actual ceremony were still bound by the terms of the covenant. The role of the covenant representative was vital, so that individual was required to have significant status and to be of the same blood as the group represented.

COMMON ELEMENTS

It seems that the basic design of a covenant was established by God from the earliest of times, but the general concept was also widely embraced by pagan cultures. Thus, the core elements were sometimes corrupted to include heinous acts such as human sacrifice. Our challenge is to sift through the "dirt" of misguided behavior so we might better understand and embrace our Creator's perspective of this vital concept.

---

9. Kline, *Kingdom Prologue*, 3.

The Bible was penned in the Middle East, and most ancient covenants from that region fit a basic form of shared elements. The order might have varied, but the format was usually similar:

- A preamble
- A historical introduction
- A list of stipulations
- Oaths (often with witnesses)
- Blessings and curses
- A shared meal
- A seal or memorial reminder of the covenant
- A religious ceremony, often with blood

Considering the elements of an ancient covenant reminds us that the concept is both familiar and strange. We see vestiges of an ancient covenant, for example, in the vows, rings, and celebratory meals of marriage ceremonies. At the same time, many elements, particularly those involving animal sacrifices and blood, are foreign to our Western mindsets.

The preamble and historical introduction established which parties were involved and also shared a little about the history of their relationship. A list of stipulations then laid out the terms of the covenant, which were supported by solemn oaths given by both parties. In ancient cultures, these oaths constituted *a legal, binding agreement.* An example from a pre-Mohammad Middle-Eastern covenant reads:

> The brother [in such a covenant] must guard the [other] brother from treachery, and [must] succor him in peril. So far as may be necessary, the one must provide for the wants of the other; and the survivor has weighty obligations in behalf of the family of the one deceased.[10]

---
10. Trumbull, *The Blood Covenant*, 10.

A covenant-friend, in ancient times, was much like a sibling and very different from the social media friends that people accumulate today. A friend, in a covenantal sense, was no distant acquaintance, but rather a loyal and trusted brother. Blessings were pronounced for those who honored the terms of the covenant, and vile curses were proclaimed upon those who stooped low enough to break them. There is plenty of cursing on social media, of course, but it is of a very different sort!

The nineteenth-century explorer, Henry M. Stanley, made numerous covenants with African tribal chiefs as he traveled throughout that vast, primitive territory. Making "strong friendship" or becoming a "blood brother" with a powerful chief provided both safety and provision for Stanley and his crew. But there were also stark warnings about breaking the sacred oaths. Henry Clay Trumbull highlights a late nineteenth-century covenant ceremony between Stanley and the great African chief Mirambo:

> Having caused us to sit fronting each other on a straw-carpet, he made an incision in each of our right legs, from which he extracted blood, and inter-changing it, he exclaimed aloud: "If either of you break this brotherhood now established between you, may the lion devour him, the serpent poison him, bitterness be in his food, his friends desert him, his gun burst in his hands and wound him, and everything that is bad do wrong to him until death."[11]

After the solemnity had finished, everyone celebrated the covenant by sharing a meal—commonly an animal that had been sacrificed during the ceremony. The profound connection between food and interpersonal relationships, it seems, has been part of our human experience from time immemorial.

The parties sometimes exchanged gifts and also established a means of remembering the covenant so that it was always near to their hearts and minds. The memorial might have been a pile of stones, the terms of the covenant carried in a leather amulet, or the

---

11. Trumbull, *Blood Covenant*, 20.

permanent dark scars left from mixing gunpowder with blood at the place of an incision. Remembering the covenant was vital because it was considered to be sacred and binding for the coming generations.

Because of the high degree of commitment required, covenant ceremonies often took place with the participants' deities in mind. Within an environment of deep religious belief, vows before God were the weightiest of all. In most ancient covenants, blood was also used—either the blood of a sacrifice for sprinkling or drinking, or the blood of two individuals commingled together.

LIFE AND DEATH

The term "cutting a covenant" was frequently used to describe the initiation of a covenant relationship in ancient times. Many scholars believe that it signified the cutting of a sacrificial animal. And during Middle-Eastern covenant ceremonies, it was also common for the participants to walk between the sacrificed animals in the form of a figure eight. This physical act proclaimed a powerful message: "May I become like one of these sacrificed animals if I break our pact!"

Why do participants in covenants make oaths? Because so much is at stake. Every covenant requires some manner of death (see Hebrews 9:16). Like extinguishing two separate flames and lighting a unity candle at a wedding, parts of the covenant ceremony symbolize death to an old existence as two parties enter into a new, unified life together. With a sacred covenant, old self-oriented lifestyles must give way for a new partnership to flourish.

The book of Hebrews provides several stark reminders of the dangers of treating a covenant with God casually or irreverently (Hebrews 2:1-2; 3:7-11; 6:1-8; 10:26-31; 12:25-29). The issue is heavy and might seem overdone to those who lack a covenantal mentality. What is not overdone, however, is the sense of security we find when we grasp the reality of being in covenant with the all-powerful Creator of our cosmos.

A blood covenant was considered to be especially sacred in ancient times. According to Trumbull:

> The root idea of this rite of blood-friendship seems to include the belief, that the blood is the life of a living being; not merely that the blood is essential to life, but that, in a peculiar sense, it is life; that it actually vivifies by its presence; and that by its passing from one organism to another it carries and imparts life. The inter-commingling of the blood of two organisms is, therefore, according to this view, equivalent to the inter-commingling of the lives, of the personalities, of the natures, thus brought together; so that there is, thereby and thenceforward, one life in two bodies, a common life between the two friends.[12]

Trumbull's statement reflects an ancient mindset that played largely into the Jewish faith and profoundly influences our current Christianity as well: *the life of the flesh is in the blood.*

> "For the life of the flesh is in the blood, and I have given it to you on the altar to make atonement for your souls; for it is the blood by reason of the life that makes atonement." Leviticus 17:11

Blood was often incorporated into covenant ceremonies because of the desire for *renewed vitality*. And again, while the core elements of this mindset are rooted in Biblical truth, many ancient cultures corrupted the concept to create heinous practices such as drinking the blood or eating the heart and liver of a newly slain foe, with the hopes of receiving his strength and valor.

The practice of sacrificing animals to make amends for human sins links to the idea that the life present in an animal's blood would cover the death resulting from a person's transgressions. A key element in this thought process was *innocence*. Possessing no moral capacity, animals such as sheep and goats were considered to be guilt free, and so their blood was unstained by the corruption embodied in human sinfulness.

---

12. Trumbull, *The Blood Covenant*, 38.

While our modern view of ancient sacrificial practices often focuses on death, the ancient intent was to receive *life* in its full vitality. Through the life of the blood, intimate union with God (or the gods) and man were thought to be possible. And though their efforts were wildly misguided, becoming one with God seemed to be the ultimate goal of even the ancient pagans. Trumbull continues:

> A covenant of blood, a covenant made by the inter-commingling of blood, has been recognized as the closest, the holiest, and the most indissoluble, compact conceivable. Such a covenant clearly involves an absolute surrender of one's separate self, and an irrevocable merging of one's individual nature into the dual, or the multiplied, personality included in the compact. Man's highest and noblest outreachings of soul, have, therefore, been for such a union with the divine nature as is typified in this human covenant of blood.[13]

Developing a clearer understanding of ancient covenantal mindsets enables us to better understand the divine logic behind the Christian faith. Otherwise, the apparent cruelty of the "Old Testament God" will sow seeds of doubt and tempt us to reject the inspired, infallible, and authoritative nature of the Bible. I have even heard some pastors claim that we need to move beyond "a grotesque emphasis on blood and sacrifice" in our understanding of the Christian faith. That would be a mistake of epic proportions! We dare not twist the Scriptures to conform to our cultural trends. Rather, we must align ourselves with our Creator's design—one that is embodied in a covenantal mindset.

WRAP-UP

The Bible is rich with meaning, but we can only mine the depths of its treasures as we step outside the boundaries of modern cultural thought. Yes, ancient covenants were agreements, but they were also very different from the business contracts of our modern era. The old Gecho chief called establishing a covenant "drinking truth" because

---
13. Trumbull, *The Blood Covenant*, 204.

it carried an uncommon degree of faithful devotion. As we continue to plumb the depths of Scripture in a covenantal context, more and more, we will grasp the genius of our Creator's loving design for the human race.

Many covenant ceremonies incorporated blood sacrifices, and the image of the innocent animals being killed for their vitality points toward a much greater spiritual reality: *the life-blood of the perfect and eternal Son of God has the power to cleanse even the worst human sins and redeem us from certain death.* While some people see the concept of sacrificial blood as grotesque, Christ's sacrificial death on the cross also displays a profound beauty. We will explore this concept in further detail at a later point, but for now, I want to communicate more than a history lesson: *the covenantal mindset of ancient times is embodied within Biblical Christianity.*

DISCUSSION

1. Share an example of a covenant story from a book or movie.
2. If you can, give an example of a covenant in modern-day life.
3. How does a covenant-friend differ from a social media friend?
4. Why are vows and oaths involved with covenants?
5. According to Leviticus 17:11, what purpose does a blood sacrifice fulfill?
6. Please comment on the following statement: *The Bible is first and foremost a book of relationship.*

Chapter Two

THE HEART OF GOD'S COVENANTS

*He has remembered His covenant forever,
The word which He commanded to a thousand generations.*
                                                        Psalm 105:8

A group is as healthy as its "social contract" is clear; a congregation as faithful as its covenant is mutually understood; a pastor as effective as the pastor's and people's commitment to trust and integrity is honored, guarded, and fulfilled.

—David Augsburger

"What loving person would want to serve a God who orders the genocide of innocent women and children?" Such might be a typical query used to cast doubt upon the credibility of the Biblical God. Criticizing what we do not understand comes easily—my weed-eater story from the Introduction proved that to be true in my life.

Critics of Christianity often point toward the Old Testament to justify their rejection of the Bible, and thus, the authority of the God who authored it. The Old Testament is a fascinating document—full of dramatic events, seemingly bloodthirsty actions, and cultural mindsets very different from ours. For those raised in a culture devoid of covenantal thinking, criticisms of that ancient document might seem to flow within the winds of reason. However, if we can grasp the mindset of the time, along with the purposes of the Old Testament, even stories that grieve our hearts will begin to reveal a divine logic.

From a Christian perspective, the primary purpose of the Old Testament is to help set the stage for the New Testament. The physical examples and representations (often called "types") found in Genesis through Malachi illuminate the eternal spiritual concepts found in Matthew through Revelation. Without the former, the latter would make little sense.

The Old Testament also serves as a compass of sorts. From start to finish, its pages point us toward a greater reality: the arrival of Jesus Christ—God in human flesh—on planet Earth. Failing to understand this purpose leads us to focus our attention on the mechanics of the compass, criticizing and deriding its validity, while forgetting about the direction in which it points. Furthermore, Jesus was born into a Jewish covenant culture. To interpret His teachings through a Western mindset, without understanding the culture in which He lived, can be like trying to participate in a sporting event without knowing how the game is played.

This point about culture proved true several years ago when Debi and I hosted a college student from China. Due to our cultural differences, plenty of confusion was had by all. Then, after building a relationship for several months, his wife arrived in the States, and the cultural learning process began all over again.

Once, we took Limin and Goya to a traditional local diner— the kind that gray-haired Americans frequent. As Debi and I ate our salads, the young Asian couple could not stop laughing. Covering their mouths in a vain attempt to be polite, they kept smiling and whispering to one another in Mandarin. Their explanation? In their homeland, no one eats raw vegetables. Our common garden salad was their cultural oddity. If such a scenario can take place among modern contemporaries, what are the challenges for people groups separated by not just geography, but also by thousands of years? As Christians, we must at least acknowledge the importance of cultural history.

ONENESS

The core of the Old Testament is formed by the old covenant. Apart from the book of Genesis, most of the Old Testament revolves around the covenant that God established with Israel through the giving of the Mosaic law.

Numerous aspects of the Mosaic law remain foreign to Western thought, but if we can sift through the confusion, we will see God's eternal plan on grand display. We want to move beyond the peripheral issues to grasp the Lord's heart, to lay hold of both His passion and the central mindset that characterizes His relationship with humanity.

Considering the establishment of the old covenant, as found in the book of Exodus and spread out over chapters 19–24, we can identify the covenant elements presented in our previous chapter:

- Preamble (Exodus 20:2a) - "I am the Lord your God,"

- Historical introduction (Exodus 20:2b) - "who brought you out of Egypt, out of the land of slavery."

- List of stipulations (Exodus 20:3–17) - The Ten Commandments

- Blessings and curses (Exodus 20:5–6) - "I, the Lord your God, am a jealous God, visiting the iniquity of the fathers on the children, on the third and the fourth generations of those who hate Me, but showing lovingkindness to thousands, to those who love Me and keep My commandments."

- Oaths (Exodus 24:3) - "When Moses went and told the people all the Lord's words and laws, they responded with one voice, 'Everything the Lord has said we will do.'"

- A memorial (Exodus 24:4b) - "He got up early the next morning and built an altar at the foot of the mountain and set up twelve stone pillars representing the twelve tribes of Israel."

- A religious ceremony with blood (Exodus 24:5-6) - "He sent young men of the sons of Israel, and they offered burnt offerings and sacrificed young bulls as peace offerings to the Lord. Moses took half of the blood and put it in basins, and the other half of the blood he sprinkled on the altar."

- A shared meal (Exodus 24:9-11) - "Moses and Aaron, Nadab and Abihu, and the seventy elders of Israel went up and saw the God of Israel . . . But God did not raise his hand against these leaders of the Israelites; they saw God, and they ate and drank."

As we can see, the old covenant closely followed the basic pattern of Middle-Eastern covenants of that day. Furthermore, a key purpose of the Mosaic covenant was to establish a oneness relationship between the Lord and His covenant people. Looking into Exodus 25, we read:

> There I will meet with you; and from above the mercy seat, from between the two cherubim which are upon the ark of the testimony, I will speak to you about all that I will give you in commandment for the sons of Israel. Exodus 25:22

This promise, given by God to Moses, was what the ancients longed to hear! The nation of Israel—the progeny of Abraham and Sarah, whom we will meet in chapter four—was being given the opportunity to enter into a mystical union with the Divine. It was God who initiated this covenant as He met with the people of Israel in their cultural paradigm.

Exodus 25:10-22 describes the design for the *Ark of the Covenant*—a wooden, gold-plated box where the manifest presence of God would dwell. Covering the Ark was a golden "mercy seat" that would be sprinkled with sacrificial blood on the holiest day of the Jewish year—*Yom Kippur*. This day is known as the "Day of Atonement," and a new word—*atonement*—was coined by the English to describe its meaning:

> *Atonement*, which was first used in a religious sense, actually meant "at-one-ment." Early authors were wont to write the phrase "to make a *onement* with God," meaning to be reconciled with God, to be united with Him and at peace . . . *One*, at that time, was pronounced much like our modern word "own" and this accounts for the present pronunciation of *atone*, although as far as the sense is concerned, we might just as well say *at one*.[1]

The concept of becoming one with God is both fascinating and mysterious. Humans do not become gods; instead, we enter into a spiritual union *with* God. Though we might struggle to explain such a mysterious connection with our Creator, He has always desired deep intimacy with us. Ultimately, Jesus atoned for our sins so that we might be "at one" with the God who fills us with the breath of life.

Through the Old Testament, we see the formation of a sacrificial system within a covenantal worldview. The various types of sacrifices help us grasp the majesty of Jesus' death and resurrection, while the covenant concept gives us deeper insight into God and His ways. *The Lord of our universe does not need covenants to bind Him to His word, but we need them to help us understand the depths of His character.*

With these things in mind, we will now consider two Old Testament covenants: Israel's treaty with the Gibeonites and David's covenant with Jonathan. Through these stories, we catch a powerful glimpse of two key virtues that characterize sacred covenants: *faithfulness* and *lovingkindness*. We will begin with faithfulness.

ISRAEL'S TREATY WITH THE GIBEONITES

The treaty between Israel and Gibeon provides an excellent example of a suzerain-vassal covenant where a more powerful nation sets the terms for a weaker one (Joshua 9). This story, however, has a significant twist that further illuminates the Lord's way of thinking.

---

1. Wilfred Funk, Litt. D., *Word Origins: An Exploration and History of Words and Language*, (New York, Wings Books. Published by arrangement with T.Y. Crowell Publishers, 1998), 268.

When our Creator made a covenant with Abraham (formerly Abram), He promised the man that his descendants would one day possess the land of Canaan (Genesis 13:14–17). After centuries of slavery, the Lord not only delivered those descendants from captivity in Egypt, He also began to fulfill His promise regarding the land. The newly formed nation of ragtag former slaves was soon conquering kingdoms that were far stronger and much better equipped for battle.

Filled with trembling as they watched surrounding kingdoms fall, the leaders of Gibeon hatched a deceptive plan to form a treaty with Israel. Dressed as though they had come from a far-off country, a group of Gibeonites offered to share the rich products of their land, if only they could forge a covenant relationship together. Somewhat naively, and without consulting God, Israel's leaders made the pact as requested. Three days later they discovered that the Gibeonites were a neighboring kingdom—but the covenant had already been made.

Burning with fury, the people of Israel wanted to destroy the Gibeonites for their deceit. Joshua and his leaders, however, refused to violate a covenant that they saw as sacred in the eyes of God.

> But all the leaders said to the whole congregation, "We have sworn to them by the Lord, the God of Israel, and now we cannot touch them." Joshua 9:19

An oath before God was considered a sacred pact, so instead of killing the Gibeonites, Israel's leaders put them to work cutting wood and hauling water. In no way would they harm the deceitful liars.

Not long after the covenant was established, a group of hostile kings, infuriated by the new alliance, attacked the Gibeonites. A messenger soon pleaded with Joshua, "Do not abandon your servants; come up to us quickly and save us and help us, for all the kings of the Amorites that live in the hill country have assembled against us" (Joshua 10:6b).

Consider the situation. Here was a nation of deceivers asking the men of Israel to risk their lives to defend them. What was Joshua's response? Without delay, he marched his men all night long to confront the enemy kings and their armies in battle. I would have been tempted to set out the next morning after a hearty breakfast.

A person might be inclined to wonder how God felt about the covenant between Israel and Gibeon. Was He angry that His people would take such a risk? Or was He somehow pleased that they would put themselves on the front lines of battle for a nation of deceiving scoundrels? The answer was clear as crystal. Not only did the Lord throw large hailstones from heaven to defeat those armies, He also caused the sun to stand still for several hours, while Joshua and his men finished the battle (Joshua 10:11-14).

> There was no day like that before it or after it, when the Lord listened to the voice of a man [Joshua]; for the Lord fought for Israel. Joshua 10:14

What can we glean from this incredible story? Even though the Israelites were deceived into making a treaty, they honored its terms by risking their lives to rescue the Gibeonites. Furthermore, God honored Israel's faithfulness to the covenant by taking extreme actions to help them with the fight. The Creator of our vast universe did not care about the false pretenses under which the covenant was established. Instead, He honored the request of Joshua—one of the leaders who proclaimed, "We have sworn to them by the Lord, the God of Israel, and now we cannot touch them." On that day, God performed an unthinkable miracle by causing the sun to stand still in the sky. The story, however, does not end there.

Somewhere between two hundred and four hundred years later, Israel's King Saul—a man who seemed to have little regard for covenant faithfulness—killed some of the Gibeonites. God's displeasure was later revealed by a famine that came upon Israel as a result of the broken treaty. Only after Israel turned over seven of Saul's descendants to the Gibeonites to be killed did the famine abate (2 Samuel 21:1-14). Even the passage of time—hundreds of years in this case—failed to erode the sanctity of Israel's covenant with Gibeon.

Israel's penalty for breaking its vow might seem harsh to us, but it communicates the power of a covenant bond. Neither a deceitful beginning, nor the passing centuries, could diminish the strength of a sacred oath. Covenants made before God do not have expiration dates. If we are to understand the covenants of the Bible, and especially the new covenant, we must develop this type of mindset. *Casual participation in a covenant relationship is a concept that does not exist.*

FAITHFULNESS

Those who enter into a sacred and binding covenant are expected to be faithful to its terms regardless of the cost involved. This aspect of a covenant relationship reflects God's faithfulness, which, according to the Psalmist, "reaches to the skies."

> Your lovingkindness, O Lord, extends to the heavens,
> Your faithfulness reaches to the skies.
> Psalm 36:5

Are we talking about a specific distance? I think not. God's faithfulness extends into the heavens so far that grasping its full extent is beyond our reach.

The Hebrew word for faithfulness here is *emunah*, which is connected to the more commonly known "amen." *Emunah* can also mean *faithfulness, steadiness, honesty, security,* or *truth*.[2] Thus, we can say that *God's faithfulness is the stable and secure reality of our lives.*

Faithfulness is essential for meaningful relationships. When I was young, we had a common saying: "A man's word is his bond." In that era, it was not uncommon for a major business deal to be sealed with a mere handshake. Today, fewer and fewer people seem to be faithful to their word. We need everything "in writing," and even then there is no guarantee it will be honored. We do not know whom to trust anymore, and so we find ourselves frustrated, angry,

---

2. James Swanson, *Dictionary of Biblical Languages with Semantic Domains: Hebrew (Old Testament)* (Oak Harbor: Logos Research Systems, Inc., 1997).

and anxious. Indeed, many of the cataclysmic problems we face in Western society are the direct results of mistrust.

In whom do you put your trust? Politicians? Business executives? Academic experts? Religious leaders? Yourself? History has given us reason to doubt them all. But life was never meant to be this way! Perhaps some aspects of being "old-fashioned" are not so bad.

Reaching into the ancient covenantal mindset, both elected and appointed U.S. government officials must still take an oath of office:

> I do solemnly swear (or affirm) that I will support and defend the Constitution of the United States against all enemies, foreign and domestic; that I will bear true faith and allegiance to the same; that I take this obligation freely, without any mental reservation or purpose of evasion; and that I will well and faithfully discharge the duties of the office on which I am about to enter: So help me God.[3]

By taking an oath before God, government servants enter into a covenant relationship with their nation. But sadly, we hear far too many stories of political corruption when, based on their sacred oaths, elected government officials should be some of the people we trust most. Thankfully, we still have a standard of ethics—at least in principle. In some nations, political corruption runs rampant, destroying any sense of stability and hope for a better tomorrow.

When mistrust becomes a part of the social fabric, a nation loses heart. Without trust, injustice reigns, and people become increasingly anxious, depressed, and hopeless. These negative emotions then exacerbate other social problems such as violence, substance abuse, and suicide.

College administrators, in recent years, have seen a significant increase in emotional disorders among incoming students. Why? Why are so many of our young adults seemingly less equipped to deal

---

3. U.S. Senate: Oath of Office, accessed October 22, 2019, https://www.senate.gov/artandhistory/history/common/briefing/Oath_Office.htm.

with the realities of life than previous generations? Why are they so anxious and unstable? Many factors are at play, but a primary cause is that they have been born into a world they cannot trust.

We are tempted to lay all the blame on those young people, but past icons of security have shown themselves unworthy of trust, and thanks to technological advances, our youth are well aware. They no longer believe when a company says that safety is their highest priority (as though making money did not matter). They look with skepticism when religious leaders proclaim to follow in the footsteps of Jesus (as though covering up child abuse is something He would have done). And they boil with cynicism when a politician broadcasts, "You can trust me!" (as though lobbyist dollars buy no influence).

In our *postmodern* era, the younger generations have also been conditioned to mistrust the concept of *absolute truth*. But apart from the absolute reality of a good and faithful God, we can have no security on this earth. None whatsoever. Without absolute truth, there can be no justice—or injustice, for that matter. Much of the outrage, fear, and anxiety we see all around us are rotten fruits of a postmodern world.

The Lord's faithfulness is absolute. It is our understanding that is limited. There is no difference between a spoken word, a promise, or an oath from God. The Almighty says what He means, and means what He says. When we cannot trust anyone, we can trust God.

I do not know how some people do it. To live apart from our Creator's absolute reality is to run adrift on a tumultuous sea. With no anchor and no security, with no one to lean into when storm-driven waves crash—such is the sad and depressing state of a life without God. When circumstances go awry, I want more than positive thoughts and warm platitudes; I need an unmovable Rock of stability.

Regardless of what happens around us—or to us—we can be at peace as we trust the Lord even through the darkest circumstances. Such "God-confidence" helps us navigate the dangerous shoals of modern life. And just as important, as we learn to trust Him in greater measures, we become more trustworthy—a transformation that has a powerful ripple effect on the world around us.

If we want peace, security, and healthy relationships, trust is not optional. That trust, however, is impossible to establish if we ourselves are not faithful to our word. A similar principle applies to our relationship with God. Not only must we learn to trust Him, we also must be people He can trust.

The ancient Jewish concept of *righteousness* was closely linked to how the Hebrews treated one another, being interwoven with their trustworthiness.

> O Lord, who may abide in Your tent?
> Who may dwell on Your holy hill?
> He who walks with integrity, and works righteousness,
> And speaks truth in his heart.
> He does not slander with his tongue,
> Nor does evil to his neighbor,
> Nor takes up a reproach against his friend;
> In whose eyes a reprobate is despised,
> But who honors those who fear the Lord;
> He swears to his own hurt and does not change.
> Psalm 15:1–4

The final line, in particular, shouts out the importance of trustworthiness. When a man makes a covenant oath, he is expected to stand by his word regardless of the personal cost. *Those who drink truth will speak and live truth.* Such integrity then becomes the foundation upon which a healthy tribe of people functions.

The Lord seeks to do awesome feats in our midst, but He chooses to work through people. Herein lies one of the great mysteries of the universe: our perfect God uses imperfect people to accomplish awesome eternal purposes. This mysterious approach creates a multitude of problems that would not exist if God accomplished His work by Himself or through angels. But our all-powerful Lord is up to the task as He transforms those who put their trust in Him. Even our faithfulness need not be perfect. The man or woman who grows, day by day, to be trustworthy will be used powerfully by our Master.

OUR STEADFAST LORD

A Christian's ability to live faithfully in an unfaithful world proceeds from the very throne of heaven. It is God's steadfast and true character that enables us to grow as faithful stewards of His gracious gifts. Furthermore, reaching our full potential begins with a revelation of His stellar and steadfast character. Only as we see Him for who He is can we become who we were destined to be.

More than raw power is at work with our sovereign King. The Lord's faithfulness comes from a unique mix of power and integrity. He is sovereign over all, so no person or situation can cause Him to be unfaithful. He is entirely whole, with no brokenness or flaw in His character. The Almighty God is not beset by the same frailties of will that plague the common human. He will be faithful to His promises, without question and without fail. This truth is the eternal reality upon which the universe is founded, and the anchor that brings stability to our storm-tossed lives.

Not long ago, I missed a meeting. My intentions were not the issue. While I fully intended to be there, I became sidetracked with incoming texts, messages, and a visit; plenty of things needed my attention after a week's vacation. Nothing of the sort will ever happen with the God who created our universe. He is *never* forgetful, or sidetracked, or delayed. Do not expect to see the Lord sitting stuck in traffic, brimming with frustration, and blaring His horn—ever!

God is trustworthy in every way possible; there has never been a time when He was unfaithful. But sadly, humanity has had a difficult time grasping the weight of divine goodness. Have you read about Eden? As recorded in Genesis 3:1, the very first words from the serpent's mouth called the Lord's trustworthiness into question. "Indeed, has God said, 'You shall not eat from any tree of the garden'?" Humans have doubted God ever since, and our unbelief is killing us.

A primary reason that the Lord established the concept of covenant is to give us a tangible context from which to grasp the depths of His absolute and unwavering faithfulness. When I talk with other Christians about covenants, for example, they often nod their heads in affirmation. But when I begin to share the story of Israel and the Gibeonites, mental light bulbs begin to burn bright. This covenant example gives life to the understanding of God's faithfulness—it ceases to be a nebulous idea and becomes a tangible reality instead.

LOVINGKINDNESS

Lovingkindness, the second key virtue that characterizes covenants, can be found displayed in the story of Jonathan (a crown prince) and David (a lowly shepherd).

> Now it came about when he had finished speaking to Saul, that the soul of Jonathan was knit to the soul of David, and Jonathan loved him as himself. Saul took him that day and did not let him return to his father's house. Then Jonathan made a covenant with David because he loved him as himself. Jonathan stripped himself of the robe that was on him and gave it to David, with his armor, including his sword and his bow and his belt. 1 Samuel 18:1–4

The price that Jonathan paid to form this bond stretches the depths of our imaginations. His father was grooming the young man to be the next king of Israel, but in forging this covenant with David, Jonathan chose to forfeit the glory and power that so often captivate human passions. Furthermore, by giving David his robe and weapons, the crown prince surrendered to a shepherd part of his identity. When people saw David wearing Jonathan's robe and carrying his weapons, they understood that he was a covenant-friend of the king's son.

Circumstances did not develop as expected, and King Saul burned with jealousy toward David—to the point of hurling a spear at the young man. But because of their covenant bond, Jonathan spurned his father's animosity and remained loyal to David. Full-blown tragedy then struck. Saul and Jonathan, along with several members of their royal family, were slain in battle. David wept with grief, but their deaths also put him in a position to become king and unify the nation.

UNDERBELLY LOVE

As we read in 2 Samuel 9:1, after the new king solidified his power, he asked an unlikely question: "Is there yet anyone left of the house of Saul, that I may show him kindness for Jonathan's sake?" Why such a response? The two men once drank truth together. David's faithful desires could not help but seek expression through practical love.

The Hebrew word *hesed*—translated in 2 Samuel 9:1 as "kindness"—is rich with meaning and frequently used (almost 250 times) throughout the Old Testament. The depth of meaning is difficult for us to grasp because the word does not translate well into English. Various Bible versions translate *hesed* as "mercy," "love," "faithfulness," "lovingkindness," "steadfast love," "faithful love," and "unfailing love."

In essence, *hesed* means to freely show kindness to a person who is somehow connected through a prior relationship.[4] There are times when we might feel an awkward obligation to help someone in need. We stutter and stammer, trying to find a gracious way to avoid getting involved. That is not *hesed*.

I once had an acquaintance who asked to borrow my car so that he could drive it into the city. Uncomfortable with the idea, I politely declined. But afraid of seeming "un-Christian," I offered to drive him. My heart was not in my offer, and so the experience felt like returning to a miserable job on Monday morning—only it lasted all day. Many years later, my daughter needed help moving in that very same city. Not only did I gladly make the drive, I spent the better part of a day carrying furniture up and down multiple flights of steps. Yes, the hard work exhausted me, but in the depths of my heart I wanted to bless my own flesh and blood.

---

4. R. Laird Harris, "698 חסד," ed. R. Laird Harris, Gleason L. Archer Jr., and Bruce K. Waltke, *Theological Wordbook of the Old Testament* (Chicago: Moody Press, 1999), 307.

Hesed is a devoted love that forever seeks opportunities to help and bless. It is the loyal love we all long for, knowing that someone will stand with us and look out for our well-being in good times and in bad. We might call *hesed* "underbelly love" because there is nothing like being loved by those who have seen the worst of you and yet remain faithful.

Regardless of whether *hesed* is the motivation for a person to enter a covenant, or whether it is the fruit of a covenant relationship, the concept is well-exemplified by King David. "Is there yet anyone left of the house of Saul, that I may show him kindness [*hesed*] for Jonathan's sake?"

MEPHIBOSHETH

The answer to King David's question was, "Yes!" On the day that Saul and Jonathan were slain on Mount Gilboa, Jonathan's five-year-old son was accidentally dropped on the ground by a nurse fleeing to protect him. The boy became permanently crippled in a masculine, warring culture. His name had been Meribbaal, which has an uncertain meaning. But as the king's grandson, you can be sure that the name was lofty (*baal* means "lord"). Sometime after that ill-fated day, his name was changed to *Mephibosheth*, which some scholars believe means "from the mouth of shame."[5]

Mephibosheth appeared before the king of Israel trembling with fear. In a move that surely immersed the palace in intrigue, David gave Mephibosheth the highest honor of dining at the king's table, treating him like a son. The king also restored Mephibosheth's inheritance, giving him all the property that had belonged to his grandfather Saul.

What was Mephibosheth's response to David's unusual kindness? The young man prostrated himself, saying, "What is your servant, that you should regard a dead dog like me?" (2 Samuel 9:8b). Mephibosheth thoroughly understood the dynamics of his situation. Broken and disgraced, Saul's grandson knelt before the mighty king

---

5. Reader's Digest Association, *Who's Who in the Bible* (Pleasantville, NY: Reader's Digest, 1994), 293.

of Israel, having nothing to offer except potential competition for the royal throne.

David's kindness to Mephibosheth was no random act of kindness or senseless act of beauty. He was expressing heartfelt love toward his dear friend Jonathan, and that love provides a powerful picture of God's heart toward us. The king extended grace to his potential enemy because he grasped the depths of God's *hesed*. Throughout the Psalms, we find David struggling with extreme adversity but always returning His gaze to the Lord's goodness. The final verse of the much-loved Psalm 23 provides us with an awesome example of David's insight:

> Surely your goodness and unfailing love [*hesed*] will pursue [chase after] me all the days of my life, and I will live in the house of the Lord forever. Psalm 23:6 (NLT)

Through an extended enrollment at *Adversity University*, the former shepherd came to understand that God's unfailing love doggedly pursues His covenant children through every season of their lives. Due to our limited vision, however, we do not always understand how the Lord's faithful love influences our daily lives, which is why we need to trust both His character and His Word. David, along with many other ancients, learned that:

> The Lord is gracious and merciful;
> Slow to anger and great in lovingkindness [*hesed*].
> Psalm 145:8

Faithfulness and lovingkindness—both are powerful dimensions of God's character that He has interwoven into the tapestry of His covenants. Are these not two of the primary qualities that we all long for in our relationships? Do we not desire friends and family members who will stand faithful regardless of the personal cost, people who cherish us in their hearts and seek to bless us in thoughtful ways?

It is impossible to analytically separate God's faithfulness from His *hesed* because they are both integral to His nature. And because

THE HEART OF GOD'S COVENANTS

of who He is, we never need to fear being defrauded or abandoned by Him. Regardless of how circumstances might appear, the Lord is *always* faithful to do what He says, and His beloved children are *always* at the center of His desire to bless. *The omniscient God knows our worst and yet loves us the best.*

WRAP-UP

By immersing ourselves in the covenant stories of the Bible, we can develop a clearer understanding of our Creator. No matter what outward appearances might proclaim, He has always desired to establish a unique "oneness" relationship with His human creations.

Admittedly, there is something about a covenant union with God that does not seem right. In light of our moral failings, why would He bother? What we often fail to understand is that God is who He is, regardless of who we are and what we do. The Lord's faithfulness is innate to His character. The Almighty was faithful long before we came into existence, and He remains faithful even when we are not (see 2 Timothy 2:13). There is no need for Him to "drink truth" because *He is truth.*

We might feel unworthy, but that means nothing to our heavenly Father. The story of King David's kindness toward Jonathan's son is in the Bible for a reason. We are all Mephibosheths. And though we have nothing to offer heaven's King except competition for His throne, He seats us at His royal table because of Christ's sacrifice on our behalf (see Ephesians 2:1–7). This is the kindness that the King of Glory extends toward "dead dog sinners" like us through the new covenant.

DISCUSSION

1. Explain how the Old Testament serves as a compass.
2. What purpose did the Ark of the Covenant serve?
3. What powerful lesson does the story of Israel's treaty with the Gibeonites communicate?

4. What problems are created by abandoning truth as an absolute?
5. Talk about some of the consequences of a lack of trust in our world.
6. Please read Ephesians 2:1-7. How does this passage relate to the story of Mephibosheth?

PART II
EARLY COVENANTS OF THE BIBLE

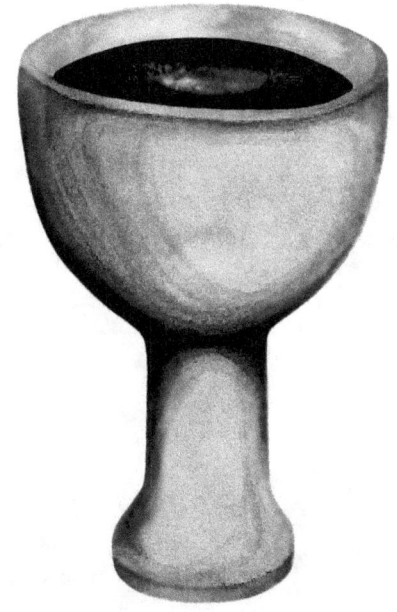

On that day the Lord made a covenant with Abram.
Genesis 15:18

Chapter Three

THE CURSED PLANET

*What more could I have done for my vineyard
   that I have not already done?
When I expected sweet grapes,
   why did my vineyard give me bitter grapes?*

Isaiah 5:4 (NLT)

I really feel like the gift is also the curse. It's always half-and-half. Whatever brings you the most joy will also probably bring you the most pain. Always a price to pay.

—Alice Hoffman

In J. R. R. Tolkien's story of Middle Earth, the King of the White Mountains—and thus the men of his realm—had sworn an oath to come to the aid of King Isildur when needed. But when that time of need arrived, the Men of the Mountains refused to honor their covenant commitment. Isildur then cursed them to have no rest until their oath was fulfilled. Despised by people of honor, they became known as the "Oathbreakers," or the "Dead Men of Dunharrow" who lingered in dark caves and made their presence known in times of trouble and death.

Like many others, Tolkien's well-crafted fantasy speaks of covenants and oaths—a storyline with roots reaching into ancient reality. That reality began in the garden of Eden, and though the word "covenant" is not used, covenantal language is present. The prophet Hosea, in speaking to the ancient nation of Israel, also referenced Adam's breaking of what is often called the "Edenic"—or "Adamic"— covenant:[1]

> But like Adam, you broke my covenant
> and betrayed my trust.
> Hosea 6:7 (NLT)

Since the beginning of history, God has related to humans—the royal children of creation—in a covenantal context. In this section, we will lay an essential foundation by highlighting five Biblical covenants. Each of these covenants plays a vital role in leading to and illuminating the greatest of all: the new covenant. Exploring the covenants found in the Old Testament will reveal fresh insights into our Christian faith.

1. The Edenic/Adamic covenant
2. The Noahic covenant
3. The Abrahamic covenant
4. The Mosaic covenant
5. The Davidic covenant

THE EDENIC/ADAMIC COVENANT

The terms of the Edenic covenant were simple. The Lord would bless and multiply Adam's lineage if humanity would obey only one stipulation: Do not eat from the tree of the knowledge of good and evil (Genesis 2:17). According to God's warning, if our ancient ancestors failed to heed His directive, they would *die*.

---

1. There is some disagreement among scholars regarding the names of several covenants and what they entail. For our purposes, I will use the terms "Edenic covenant" and "Adamic covenant" interchangeably.

In God's newly created order, humans differed significantly from the animals. Amazingly, He intended to bless humanity as the royal rulers of creation, so let us consider what that entails:

> Then God said, "Let Us make man in Our image, according to Our likeness; and let them rule over the fish of the sea and over the birds of the sky and over the cattle and over all the earth, and over every creeping thing that creeps on the earth." God created man in His own image, in the image of God He created him; male and female He created them. God blessed them; and God said to them, "Be fruitful and multiply, and fill the earth, and subdue it; and rule over the fish of the sea and over the birds of the sky and over every living thing that moves on the earth." Then God said, "Behold, I have given you every plant yielding seed that is on the surface of all the earth, and every tree which has fruit yielding seed; it shall be food for you." Genesis 1:26–29

From this short passage of Scripture, we can see that God bestowed a profound honor upon our race: *humans would reflect His very image.* Nowhere do we find similar thoughts about animals, or even angels for that matter. Long before the Lord breathed life into Adam's newly created body, He had designed a unique plan for his human lineage. Moreover, it was not just Adam who reflected the image of God, but also Eve—the woman that He formed from Adam's side. As much as our Creator wanted to be with Adam, the full richness of humanity could only be expressed in a collective sense.

The Lord also appointed humans to be *stewards* over this earth, giving them the tasks of managing His creation and exercising dominion over every living thing. This rulership aligns with God's design for planet Earth—a blueprint that finds its roots in the tree of life. And as the man and woman walked in relationship with their Creator, He would provide for their every need from the lush and abundant garden in which He placed them. Scarcity and its associated fears came later; they were never part of God's original design.

Finally, the first words the Lord spoke to His human subjects were, "Be fruitful and multiply." Though we are inclined to think of this blessing in natural terms, at that point, there was probably little separation between the spiritual and natural realms. Thus, behind the natural physical blessings of Eden, we find a profound but unseen depth of meaning that touches the core of our being.

It is difficult to imagine a more amazing beginning for humanity. The luxury of the garden proclaimed God's love for humanity, and indeed, the entire earth. In fact, the word Eden can be translated as "delight."[2] The garden was a perfectly designed and real utopia, created by God for the enjoyment of the human race. Yes, we see an overwhelming abundance of death and destruction in our current world, but we must remember that it was paradise from which we came, and to paradise that the Lord seeks to return us.

Treason and Its Consequences

Like a child enticed by a piece of candy in the hand of a stranger, Eve reached out and touched the forbidden fruit (Genesis 3:6). She did not die! Then, bringing it to her lips, she took a few curious nibbles. Emboldened by the apparent lack of consequences, Eve encouraged Adam to give it a try. Without questioning, he followed her lead. In an instant, the "van door" slammed shut, and they were captive to the lord of darkness.

At first glance, the seismic consequences brought upon the earth might seem overblown for their actions. The cumulative pain of our current and historical realities, however, makes far more sense if we dig deeper into the dynamics of what is often called "the fall." I prefer to call it "the crash" because of the overwhelming collateral damage that resulted.

To begin, Adam and Eve distrusted the most virtuous Being this universe has ever known. In doing so, the human couple placed the

---

2. Carl Schultz, "1568 עֵדֶן," ed. R. Laird Harris, Gleason L. Archer Jr., and Bruce K. Waltke, *Theological Wordbook of the Old Testament* (Chicago: Moody Press, 1999), 646.

weight of their confidence in a murderer who can do nothing but lie.[3] No matter what the devil promises, no matter how reasonable or enchanting his words might sound, the endgame is always his own selfish agenda. And we can be sure that, due to his vile nature, that agenda always involves stealing, killing, and destroying (John 10:10).

Rejecting the God who birthed them into paradise, Adam and Eve sought independence in a vain attempt to become gods themselves. Albeit unwittingly, they joined a treasonous coup against the King of Glory. Lucifer and a third of the angels had brought damnation upon themselves by seeking to violently overthrow the King of kings and Lord of lords (see Revelation 12). Without realizing the full extent of their actions—as is common for humankind—Adam and Eve committed high treason by breaking from the kingdom of heaven and aligning with murderous evil forces. We might say that they unwittingly made a covenant with the devil and that the forbidden fruit was their covenant meal.

Of all the crimes against a government, treason is the worst. The United States Code reads:

> Whoever, owing allegiance to the United States, levies war against them or adheres to their enemies, giving them aid and comfort within the United States or elsewhere, is guilty of treason and shall suffer death, or shall be imprisoned not less than five years and fined under this title but not less than $10,000; and shall be incapable of holding any office under the United States.[4]

This code was drawn from England's more extensive Treason Act that has been in place since the Middle Ages. The human race has long recognized the despicable nature of treason.

---

3. Revelation 12:9 calls Satan—the great dragon—the serpent of old. Titles such as Lucifer, Satan, the devil, the great dragon, and the serpent are all synonymous.
4. 18 U.S.C. § 2381—Treason, Sedition, and Subversive Activities, accessed October 22, 2019, https://uscode.house.gov/view.xhtml?path=/prelim@title18/part1/chapter115&edition=prelim.

By trusting the serpent over God, humanity broke a sacred covenant with their Creator and joined a treasonous rebellion against the most honorable and loving government ever to exist. In the grand scheme of the universe, our ancient ancestors committed the worst offense possible against the kingdom of light and love.

According to the Bible, the weight of Edenic guilt falls mainly on Adam because God gave the covenant command to him. Eve, however, is also guilty for her role in the debacle. Our natural response, of course, is to question why *we*, in modern times, should be held responsible for their actions.

Because we are all the products of his "seed," we were all "in" Adam when he joined the rebellion against heaven's throne. And because we were (and are) a part of Adam, all humanity owns the guilt of his actions. Even worse, we have all inherited the devil's treasonous tendencies as a result of our ancestry. Treason against God is in our nature (see Romans 5:8–10). For the most part, the term "original sin" speaks not of Adam's actions, but of the sinful tendencies inherited by those in Adam's line. *From the least to the greatest, from the cruelest to the kindest, from the vilest to the most honorable, humans are enemies of God because we ever seek to seat ourselves on His throne of power.*

A Curse and a Promise

Adam and Eve broke a sacred covenant and committed high treason against the kingdom of God. As a result, the Lord pronounced terrible curses over them and also the serpent whose enticing words drew them into rebellion. Such curses are consistent with the pain-filled consequences of violating a sacred covenant relationship.

> The Lord God said to the serpent,
>
> "Because you have done this,
> Cursed are you more than all cattle,
> And more than every beast of the field;
> On your belly you will go,
> And dust you will eat

All the days of your life;
And I will put enmity
Between you and the woman,
And between your seed and her seed;
He shall bruise you on the head,
And you shall bruise him on the heel."
Genesis 3:14–15

Like the blessings given to humanity, this curse pronounced over the serpent Satan for his role in the rebellion also has dual applications. Snakes crawl on their bellies, and many women hate them with a passion, but the spiritual being Satan also "crawls on his belly and eats dust." Furthermore, God declared that the seed of Eve—Jesus—would one day bruise the serpent's foul head. Even as the sin of Adam and Eve reverberated across creation, the Lord promised future redemption for humanity that would come through the person of Jesus Christ.

Tears of sorrow likely dripped onto the golden streets of heaven that day, but the Almighty was in no way surprised. Divine vision had foreseen the unraveling of paradise, making careful provision for its restoration. We might not understand all the happenings and consequences of the crash, but we can take comfort knowing that the Lord has long been working out a wise and loving plan for us. And as we begin to understand the dynamics of Eden's curses, we can better realize the amazing blessings that we receive through Jesus.

Woman's Curse

"Park there!" said my wife, pointing to an open space in the grocery store parking lot. "I will park *here*," I responded, "because I'm driving, and I will park where I want."

If I were to make an educated guess, I would say that Debi and I are not the only married couple to experience a bit of conflict between the genders. Much of it comes down to wrestling for control. And though such struggles are natural, they were not part of the Lord's original design.

To the woman He said,

"I will greatly multiply
Your pain in childbirth,
In pain you will bring forth children;
Yet your desire will be for your husband,
And he will rule over you."
Genesis 3:16

The pain of bearing and raising children is well-recognized, but the second part of this curse also warrants our attention. "Yet your desire will be to dominate and control your husband, and he will rule over you." That is likely what this passage communicates considering the Hebrew terminology and the context of the curse.[5] The curse pronounced over Eve has nothing to do with leadership; it is about *domination* and often plays out as a battle between the sexes.

Whether within a marriage or in a more public arena, the fight for control wreaks havoc on our social well-being. The tilt of this battle depends upon power and cunning. And while there are no clear lines to be drawn in this comparison between men and women, generalizations can sometimes be helpful. Historically, men have possessed greater physical strength, so they have controlled primarily through intimidation, force, and violence. Women, for their part, have been compelled to rely more on cunning and manipulation.

Let us say a teenager named Jimmy pesters his parents to allow him to spend a weekend at his friend's. Jimmy's father might say, "Boy, if you mention another word on the matter, I will beat your behind and lock you in your room for the weekend!" Meanwhile, the mother will take a very different approach. "Jimmy, you can go to your friends if you want, but just be aware that your poor mother will probably die from worry while you are gone. Please try to take my future grandchildren to visit their grandmother's grave every now and again."

---

5. See Genesis 4:7 and Swanson, *Dictionary of Biblical Languages with Semantic Domains: Hebrew (Old Testament)* .

Humor sometimes helps us process weighty issues, and so I joke about jostling with my wife while finding a parking space and about a mother's attempt to manipulate her son. The full reality of this ancient, pain-filled curse, however, is unpleasant in every way. We can blame men, or we can blame women, but the universal conflict between genders has deeper roots. Consider a comment made by Robert Jamieson in a nineteenth-century commentary:

> In every age of the world's history woman has been found in a state of subjection; in all heathen countries she has been the slave of man, as throughout the East at the present day she is his property—his possession by purchase.[6]

In spite of its prevalence, the male mistreatment of women was never part of God's original design. And as much as we might detest the idea of men dominating and oppressing women, females have been known to oppress males when given the power to do so. Real and lasting social harmony will be realized only as the Edenic curse is reversed through the person of Jesus Christ. If we look back over the history of our world, we will see that not only did Jesus make a radical break from the cultural oppression of women, He also initiated a system of belief that enabled women to rise to new heights.

Biblical Christianity redeems what was lost through human failure in Eden. When the gospel is understood and applied, God's good design is restored, and efforts to vie for control start dissipating. Then, as both sexes find grace to break free from the compulsion to control, women are elevated—not demeaned—in status.

Man's Curse

In essence, Adam's was a curse of *unfruitfulness*, with both natural and spiritual ramifications of exhaustion, pain, and death. Indeed,

---

6. Robert Jamieson, *A Commentary Critical, Experimental, and Practical on the Old and New Testaments,* by Robert Jamieson, A. R. Fausset, and David Brown, Volume One (Grand Rapids, MI: William B. Eerdmans Publishing Company, 1946), 58.

the curse pronounced over Adam is the antithesis of God's initial interaction with His first human son:

> God blessed them; and God said to them, "Be fruitful and multiply, and fill the earth, and subdue it; and rule over the fish of the sea and over the birds of the sky and over every living thing that moves on the earth." Genesis 1:28

Instead of fruitfulness coming easily and happily, a steep price is now paid for the ground to produce its bounty:

> Then to Adam He said, "Because you have listened to the voice of your wife, and have eaten from the tree about which I commanded you, saying, 'You shall not eat from it';

> "Cursed is the ground because of you;
> In toil you will eat of it
> All the days of your life.
> Both thorns and thistles it shall grow for you;
> And you will eat the plants of the field;
> By the sweat of your face
> You will eat bread,
> Till you return to the ground,
> Because from it you were taken;
> For you are dust,
> And to dust you shall return."
> Genesis 3:17–19

We recognize the burdensome, exhausting work required to grow food, but bearing sweet *spiritual fruit* can be just as challenging, if not more so. What do we mean by "spiritual fruit"? The apostle Paul provides a powerful description of the spiritual fruit desired by God:

> But the fruit of the Spirit is love, joy, peace, patience, kindness, goodness, faithfulness, gentleness, self-control; against such things there is no law. Galatians 5:22–23

THE CURSED PLANET

Am I saying that it is impossible for a non-Christian to genuinely love another person? Not at all. But the "thorns and thistles" of selfishness and pride cause pure love to be elusive and wrought with pain. Those who desire to cultivate noble virtues will find themselves plagued by thoughts and desires that undermine even their best intentions. A verse in Paul's letter to the Romans reflects the frustration of all humanity. Are there any among us who cannot relate?

> For the good that I want, I do not do, but I practice the very evil that I do not want. Romans 7:19

A friend of mine is a farmer. One year, he found a large portion of his field covered with bull thistle. Unlike its celebrated relative, the sunflower, this invasive, prickly weed produces nothing of value. Worse yet, one plant can produce up to 5,000 seeds in a single season. The unfortunate farmer must either apply a chemical agent or painstakingly dig out the weeds—and all their roots—by hand. For my friend, an entire growing season was lost to thorny bushes.

The bull thistle plant provides insight into an unpleasant reality: the spiritual curse of unfruitfulness. Why do we so often undermine our own hopes? Our hearts are overrun with bull thistle of the spiritual variety, and apart from a supernatural work of God within us, our efforts to change are beset by exhausting struggles.

Humanity's Plight and God's Solution

Try as we will to escape it, the death-ridden curse of Eden doggedly pursues humanity to the ends of the earth. The curse touches every marriage, every business venture, every government, indeed, every endeavor undertaken by humankind. From the highest mountain peak, to the lowest ocean depth, to the reaches of deep space, we cannot escape it. Wherever we go, the curse follows, afflicting our dreams with its deadly poison.

We might be tempted to ask why such an extreme penalty for simply eating a piece of fruit, but a covenantal mindset reminds us of how much was at stake. The human race violated a sacred trust, and trust is that important. Humans are designed to be relational beings, but when trust is lacking intimacy is made impossible. We then become self-centered isolationists, and society begins to collapse into rubble. In such an environment, social interaction becomes toxic.

Technological advances forever promise to improve our lives, but they always carry negative repercussions. A smartphone, for example, offers convenience and the ability to connect with loved ones easily, but it can also foster unhealthy addictions and miserable communications that wreak havoc on our mental health. We could list many, many more examples in our world—such as the invention of plastic—where promised blessings also carry detrimental side effects. Even our most noble pursuits will end in pain as long as the Adamic curse is in force over our race.

The prevalent reality of the curse is a difficult truth for some to accept—writing about it has not been especially pleasant either—but denial does nothing to blunt the curse's influence. Am I a defeatist? No. I just understand the ramifications of violating a sacred covenant with God. Positive thinking has its limits. Some people, for example, have riveted their focus on God's love to the point of ignoring the Adamic curse, but this blight will not simply disappear because we refuse to admit its existence.

In considering the curse, we might draw a parallel with Newton's first law of motion—often called "the law of inertia." This scientific statute tells us that a material object will remain in its current state unless acted upon by an outside force. In a similar sense, we can establish what might be called "The First Law of Biblical Covenants": *A covenant established by God—including its blessings and curses—will remain in force unless God Himself changes that covenant* (see Galatians 3:15). And if there is ever to be a change in God's dealings with the human race, He alone makes and communicates the change.

Thankfully, the Adamic curse is not the end of our story, and that is why we must continue forward in our understanding of Biblical covenants. God did make a change, and He wants that change to become reality in each of our lives. Through the sacrificial death and resurrection of Jesus, the power of the Adamic curse has been broken!

Herein, we find deeper insight into an understanding of Christian discipleship. The Lord's people are to walk with Him and grow into Christ's likeness through the transformational work of the Holy Spirit. What they learn about that process of abiding is then invested into others who can duplicate the process. In this way, the children of God are to become fruitful and multiply across the face of the earth.

Sweet spiritual fruit cannot be "manufactured" by human means but is instead the byproduct of an abiding, intimate relationship with the Lord, made possible by the new covenant in Christ's blood. Those who walk closely with their Creator will be formed by the Spirit to bear fruit for His glory (see John 15:1-11). Those who serve Him from a distance will produce rotten fruit, regardless of the outward image they portray. Other factors such as personal ability, hard work, and technology will then multiply the fruit borne, be it good or bad. No one lives without somehow influencing others.

We dare not underestimate the importance of spiritual fruitfulness! It is a thread that weaves through the Scriptures from the beginning of Genesis to the end of Revelation. Did you know that ancient Israel was rejected by her Creator because she failed to bear the spiritual fruit expected (Isaiah 5:1-7)? The same was true for many of the religious leaders in Jesus' time (Matthew 21:43). *Forming His people to bear sweet and abundant spiritual fruit continues to be at the top of God's priority list.*

THE NOAHIC COVENANT

The third chapter of Genesis ends with the tragic story of Adam and Eve being evicted from the garden of Eden—and God's presence—because of their covenant-breaking actions. The tragedy then multiplied as their firstborn son murdered his brother out of jealousy. Already, the curse of unfruitfulness was being felt. The situation only worsened from there.

By the time that Noah was born, nine generations later, the human race was distant from God, ignorant of His ways, and beset by violence.

> Then the Lord saw that the wickedness of man was great on the earth, and that every intent of the thoughts of his heart was only evil continually. The Lord was sorry that He had made man on the earth, and He was grieved in His heart. The Lord said, "I will blot out man whom I have created from the face of the land, from man to animals to creeping things and to birds of the sky; for I am sorry that I have made them." Genesis 6:5–7

The purpose of this passage is not to suggest that God was surprised by human wickedness, but to help us understand how wayward human attitudes and actions grieve His heart. The curse was bearing its rotten fruit, but the Lord had not forgotten His good plans for humanity.

Noah's father, Lamech, recognized something of God's redemptive desires in his son's birth:

> Lamech lived one hundred and eighty-two years, and became the father of a son. Now he called his name Noah, saying, "This one will give us rest from our work and from the toil of our hands arising from the ground which the Lord has cursed." Genesis 5:28–29

The name Noah means "rest," and Lamech foresaw that God wanted to use his son to alleviate the fallout from the curse of Eden.[7] We do not know how much Lamech understood about God's plans, but Genesis 6:8 tells us that "Noah found favor in the eyes of the Lord."

Angry and frustrated by human wickedness, the Lord commanded Noah to build a huge boat to save his family and each of

---

7. Leonard J. Coppes, "1323 נוּחַ," ed. R. Laird Harris, Gleason L. Archer Jr., and Bruce K. Waltke, *Theological Wordbook of the Old Testament* (Chicago: Moody Press, 1999), 562.

the animal species from a worldwide flood. Our earth, it seems, was being cleansed of wickedness and given a fresh start. The flood and the events that followed add an important step to our progression of covenants:

> Then Noah built an altar to the Lord and took some of every clean animal and some of every clean bird and offered burnt offerings on the altar. And when the Lord smelled the pleasing aroma, the Lord said in his heart, "I will never again curse the ground because of man, for the intention of man's heart is evil from his youth. Neither will I ever again strike down every living creature as I have done. While the earth remains, seedtime and harvest, cold and heat, summer and winter, day and night, shall not cease." Genesis 8:20–22 (ESV)

In Eden, innocent animals were first killed to clothe Adam and Eve. Here, Noah was sacrificing animals to help cover human sinfulness. The Hebrew word for "soothing" comes from the same root word as Noah's name, which means that the aroma was quieting, soothing, and tranquilizing—an "aroma of rest," if you will.[8] Noah's animal sacrifices enabled God to re-establish His relationship with the human race, while also pointing toward the distant sacrifice of Jesus Christ.

Within the chaos of the human wickedness and the divine judgment that it elicits, the Lord provides for us a baseline of security. The world will not run rampant or out of control; nor will God bring another devastating worldwide flood as long as we are in this era. No matter how much this planet seems to spin wildly out of control, we can rest in confidence. Just as humanity came under the curse through Adam, so will divine blessings be released to a multitude of people through Jesus the Messiah.

In the ninth chapter of Genesis, the Lord reiterates His original design for this world, while also establishing a vital truth:

---

8. Coppes, "1323 נוּחַ," ed. R. Laird Harris, Gleason L. Archer Jr., and Bruce K. Waltke, *Theological Wordbook of the Old Testament*, 562.

> And God blessed Noah and his sons and said to them, "Be fruitful and multiply and fill the earth. The fear of you and the dread of you shall be upon every beast of the earth and upon every bird of the heavens, upon everything that creeps on the ground and all the fish of the sea. Into your hand they are delivered. Every moving thing that lives shall be food for you. And as I gave you the green plants, I give you everything. But you shall not eat flesh with its life, that is, its blood. And for your lifeblood I will require a reckoning: from every beast I will require it and from man. From his fellow man I will require a reckoning for the life of man.
>
> "Whoever sheds the blood of man,
> by man shall his blood be shed,
> for God made man in his own image.
>
> "And you, be fruitful and multiply, increase greatly on the earth and multiply in it." Genesis 9:1–7 (ESV)

The blessing of fruitfulness was renewed, but the Lord also made a vital distinction between human and animal flesh. According to God's wisdom, the human race holds a unique place on earth because humans alone are created in His image.

The Lord then proclaimed the rainbow to be a memorial to the covenant that He established with Noah and the creatures over which humanity rules. Never again will there be a flood of judgment that overruns the entire earth. This "covenant of rest," established by God and confirmed by the rainbow, is an unconditional, unilateral covenant. In other words, God will bring about its fulfillment regardless of what we do or do not do.

We should not overlook another vital lesson from Noah's story. Looking back over human history, we can see that the great flood turned out to be little more than a "soft restart." It did nothing to update human nature to a more "user-friendly" version. Even the lineage of the best men and women can turn sour. In this, the Noahic covenant also points us toward the new covenant:

> For Christ also died for sins once for all, the just for the unjust, so that He might bring us to God, having been put to death in the flesh, but made alive in the spirit; in which also He went and made proclamation to the spirits now in prison, who once were disobedient, when the patience of God kept waiting in the days of Noah, during the construction of the ark, in which a few, that is, eight persons, were brought safely through the water. Corresponding to that, baptism now saves you—not the removal of dirt from the flesh, but an appeal to God for a good conscience—through the resurrection of Jesus Christ, who is at the right hand of God, having gone into heaven, after angels and authorities and powers had been subjected to Him. 1 Peter 3:18-22

In the salvation of Noah and his family, we see the picture of salvation from judgment and wrath that God is bringing to His children through the new covenant in Christ. Meanwhile, those outside the covenant will continue to languish under the Adamic curse of death and unfruitfulness.

WRAP-UP

Is the issue of the Adamic curse heavy and painful to navigate? Absolutely! But attempting to ignore its reality will do nothing to improve our situation. The indelible stain of the curse will not vanish just because we deny its presence. Yes, drinking truth can be painful, but the Lord of salvation promises genuine and lasting freedom to those who fully embrace His reality (John 8:31-32). Rather than fixating on the collateral damage caused by humanity's Edenic crash, we want to press forward in following the progression of our Lord's ancient covenants.

If we lack a covenantal worldview, the God of the Bible can seem cruel or unjust. But as we contemplate issues such as judgment, wrath, and eternal death in light of the Biblical covenants, we can begin to comprehend how their progression leads to life beyond measure. In spite of the Adamic curse, the Bible reminds us in so many ways that an abundant and fruitful life has always been the Lord's intention for humanity.

DISCUSSION

1. Explain the role of a *steward*.
2. Why is treason the worst crime against a government?
3. What does it mean to say that all humans were "in" Adam when he sinned against God?
4. In light of the Lord's original blessing over humanity (Genesis 1:28), how does Adam's curse (Genesis 3:17–19) constitute a reaping of his choice to trust the serpent and disobey God?
5. Please read Genesis 3:16 and Genesis 4:7. How has the curse polluted the relationship between male and female genders?
6. What does the story of Noah tell us about the curse over the human race and about God's good promises for our future?

Chapter Four

ABRAHAM'S LEGACY OF FAITH

And Abram believed the Lord, and the Lord counted him as righteous because of his faith.

Genesis 15:6 (NLT)

The issue of faith is not so much whether we believe in God, but whether we believe the God we believe in.

—R. C. Sproul

My earliest memory with a father figure was of riding on a wagon behind my Uncle Mick's tractor. It was a happy time following that mechanical beast on the well-worn paths of my grandmother's farm. My only other memory of Uncle Mick is from a very different setting—the Serenko Funeral Home. His lifeless body lying in a casket meant that there would be no more tractor rides.

My earliest memory about my father involved trying to convince Mom to go to New York City to bring him home, since they had separated. That eventually happened, but the joy was short-lived. He soon became sickly and reclusive. To this day, I can recall only three happy moments in which my dad was present. A fourth was a semi-happy bus trip to see a Pittsburgh Pirates baseball game—our only father-son outing.

My dad passed from this world right around my sixteenth birthday, so technically, I did not grow up fatherless. Having lacked a fatherly influence, however, I understand the dynamics involved with growing up in such a situation. The issue is a very real one in the United States because more than one-third of our children are fatherless.[1] Almost *forty percent* of the children in our society are at increased risk to live in poverty, drop out of school, abuse drugs and alcohol, engage in premarital sex, go to prison, or commit suicide, among other things.

One of my biggest frustrations from lacking a strong and present father figure was a lack of security. I struggled to define my identity, and personal confidence eluded me. I cannot begin to tell you how often my younger self lamented the "father vacuum" that left me feeling alone and insecure. Every new endeavor was met with anxious frustration as I tried to navigate an uncertain world.

I wish I could tell you that I no longer struggle with insecurity, or a lack of confidence, or anxiety. I would be lying if I did. Not only has moving on from the negative effects of my childhood proved challenging, my ministry path has led me over a long, difficult, and often lonely road. Still, if I had to describe the experience in one word, it would likely be *discovery*. Through what has seemed like a multitude of challenges and frustrations, I have discovered a depth to God's faithfulness that runs contrary to my former sense of abandonment.

I do not think my growth would have been possible had I not begun to understand the covenantal mindset embodied by the Scriptures. We have a heavenly Father—a covenant parent—who loves us beyond measure. This concept of fatherhood is integral to Biblical Christianity, and it will redefine our existence, if we allow it.

Through my Bible reading, I also discovered a spiritual father who lived thousands of years ago. In the life of Abraham (aka Abram), we find a pattern that establishes a framework for the life of every

---

1. Claudio Sanchez, "Poverty, Dropouts, Pregnancy, Suicide: What the Numbers Say About Fatherless Kids," NPR, June 18, 2017, accessed October 23, 2019, https://www.npr.org/sections/ed/2017/06/18/533062607/poverty-dropouts-pregnancy-suicide-what-the-numbers-say-about-fatherless-kids.

Christian.[2] Abraham truly was the father of our faith—a pioneer who forged a trail of trust and obedience for us to follow.

As we consider the Lord's dealings with Abraham, we see a covenant being established over a period of several years. This *Abrahamic covenant* lays a powerful foundation, which later finds its fulfillment in the new covenant established by Jesus. As we follow Abraham's story, we want to remember that our Christian roots are in him, and that all Christians are his spiritual descendants:

> And if you belong to Christ, then you are Abraham's descendants, heirs according to promise. Galatians 3:29

Transitioning from the Old Testament to the New Testament, our primary focus changes from the physical to the spiritual realm. The promise of the new covenant is by faith, and those who respond to the gospel *in faith* become heirs to the perpetual promises that the Lord made to Abraham.

ABRAHAM'S CALL

Our journey of faith begins in the ancient city of Ur, with a man named Terah and his family living in an idolatrous environment (Genesis 11:27–32). Drastic changes take place as God calls Terah's son Abram to Himself.

> Now the Lord said to Abram, "Go from your country and your kindred and your father's house to the land that I will show you. And I will make of you a great nation, and I will bless you and make your name great, so that you will be a blessing. I will bless those who bless you, and him who dishonors you I will curse, and in you all the families of the earth shall be blessed." Genesis 12:1–3 (ESV)

---

2. We will soon see that God changes the names of Abram and his wife Sarai to Abraham and Sarah, so for the sake of convenience we will begin using the later names now.

This introductory statement, given by God, and steeped in covenantal language, sets the stage for many centuries to come. These are not simplistic, archaic ideas from another era. God's profound covenant promises also apply to Abraham's spiritual progeny living in our day. Furthermore, the Lord's pattern in dealing with our forefather is repeated time without number in the lives of those descendants.

Abraham was simply following the old, idolatrous ways of his family when the Lord interrupted his plans and initiated the relationship. Many of us can relate! Even those who decide to seek God are merely responding to the Holy Spirit's promptings. *The heavenly Father is always the initiator of our redemption.*

One might think that if God initiates, we play a minimal role in the process. And I suppose the measure of our role is indeed minimal compared to His part. Nonetheless, the Lord called Abraham to take a massive risk by stepping away from all that was close and familiar to trek into the unknown. Your God-ordained story might not take you into a foreign land, but I can promise that it will break you out of your comfort zone.

Notice, too, the subtle transition from "your" to "I and you" in the Lord's initial message to Abraham. No longer would the Creator of our vast cosmos deal with the man as an outside party; instead, he would be treated as a cherished and honored friend. God's promise to bless Abraham and make him great is also interesting. Nothing indicates that the forefather of our faith sought greatness for himself. Instead, the Lord took the initiative and promised to bless Abraham by making his name great and by making him into a great nation.

How much energy do we expend trying to make a name for ourselves, trying to prove that we are significant and important? Too often, we court approval in the eyes of those who mean nothing to us in the long term. Or, at the very least, we mean little or nothing to them. Such actions flow from what might be called "an orphaned spirit." But as we begin to see our heavenly Father for His true self, the depths of His love reveal the good desires for us that exceed even our own.

Finally, God's words to Abraham in Genesis 12:3 stop me in my tracks: "I will bless those who bless you, and him who dishonors you I will curse." This is no trite statement. *The Lord takes personal offense when people treat His covenant-friends poorly.* Even something as simple as a judgmental attitude toward one of God's own is enough to warrant the imposition of a binding curse.

I used to seethe with hatred toward people who mistreated me. I now fear for them! The cruel ones of the earth betray their ignorance when they attack God's covenant children. The consequences of their actions can reverberate for a lifetime, and possibly beyond.

I suppose that Abraham could have become self-centered and arrogant, having received such lofty treatment by the Creator of our grand cosmos. But the Lord leaves little room for inflated egos. Instead, He gave Abraham a purpose beyond himself: all the families of the earth would be blessed as a result of the man's life.

Once again, the connection to our modern faith is evident. Worldly people think that ultimate fulfillment is found through the achievement of self-centered goals. They continually come up empty, but that does not stop generation after generation from trying. God's paradigm is very different. *Our deepest fulfillment—indeed, the mark of true greatness—is found in selflessly blessing others.* Being blessed is rooted in being a blessing beyond ourselves.

MYSTERIOUS MELCHIZEDEK

Another key covenant moment is recorded at the end of Genesis 14 when Melchizedek—the king of Salem and priest of God—blesses Abraham. I will note several key thoughts from this passage:

> After his return from the defeat of Chedorlaomer and the kings who were with him, the king of Sodom went out to meet him at the Valley of Shaveh (that is, the King's Valley). And Melchizedek king of Salem brought out bread and wine. (He was priest of God Most High.) And he blessed him and said,

> "Blessed be Abram by God Most High,
> Possessor of heaven and earth;
> and blessed be God Most High,
> who has delivered your enemies into your hand!"
>
> And Abram gave him a tenth of everything.
> Genesis 14:17–20 (ESV)

First, as both king and priest, Melchizedek is a "type" of Christ in that he provides a picture of Jesus. *Salem*, in verse 18, means to be complete or sound.³ The Hebrew word for peace, *shalom*, finds its roots in the same concept. In a sense, we might say, "Melchizedek is the king of wholeness and peace"—the priest of God Most High.

Second, Melchizedek shares bread and wine—representative of a covenant meal and as a precursor to the new covenant sacrament of *communion*. Melchizedek then blesses Abraham and proclaims that it was God who defeated his enemies. Finally, Abraham gives a tenth of all that he has to Melchizedek, essentially establishing the tithe as God's means of supporting the priesthood.

In the New Testament, the writer of Hebrews uses the story of Melchizedek to help us develop a better understanding of Jesus' life and ministry (see Hebrews 7). Once again, we see how the events of the Old Testament serve as a shadow and foundation for the new and better covenant.

ABRAHAM BELIEVES GOD'S PROMISE

Genesis 15 is when it happens! By "it," I mean the seismic moment that would forever define God's relationship with His covenant people:

> After these things the word of the Lord came to Abram in a vision: "Fear not, Abram, I am your shield; your reward shall be very great." But Abram said, "O Lord God, what will you give me, for I continue childless, and the heir of my house is

---

3. Thomas, *New American Standard Hebrew-Aramaic and Greek Dictionaries: Updated Edition*.

Eliezer of Damascus?" And Abram said, "Behold, you have given me no offspring, and a member of my household will be my heir." And behold, the word of the Lord came to him: "This man shall not be your heir; your very own son shall be your heir." And he brought him outside and said, "Look toward heaven, and number the stars, if you are able to number them." Then he said to him, "So shall your offspring be." And he believed the Lord, and he counted it to him as righteousness. Genesis 15:1–6 (ESV)

In this passage, the Lord reminds Abraham of their covenant relationship, calming any fears of retribution from the five kings that he surprised and defeated in battle. Our forefather responded with the audacity to question the Lord. Unfazed by the man's gumption, God made an almost unbelievable promise. This aged, childless man would become the father of a multitude beyond number. For his part, Abraham considered God to be true to His word, and the Lord credited it to him as righteousness.

I find it difficult to overestimate the importance of this interaction between God and Abraham. *The Lord declared Abraham to be acceptable and approved because the man trusted his covenant-Friend in the midst of seemingly impossible circumstances.* Herein, we find a principle central to both Judaism and Christianity:

> "Behold, as for the proud one,
> His soul is not right within him;
> But the righteous will live by his faith."
> Habakkuk 2:4

What began with Abraham finds fulfillment in the new covenant. And from start to finish, the Creator of all things expects His covenant children to trust Him—not just for a moment, but as a way of life. We are not called to simply "have" faith as a compartmentalized aspect of our existence, but to *live by faith*. Failing to grasp this fact will often lead to an anxious and angry existence in which we fail to recognize the Lord's gracious hand through each of life's adversities. The writer of Hebrews adds:

> And without faith it is impossible to please Him, for he who comes to God must believe that He is and that He is a rewarder of those who seek Him. Hebrews 11:6

Simply professing that we believe in God has little value—it might even be self-deceiving—if we do not trust Him in times of trial. And because trust provides the foundation for intimacy, the Lord will use every circumstance—regardless of the source—to create a "spiritual incubator" in which He perfects our faith. Such trust enables us to align with Him and abide in His grace, thus producing a bountiful harvest of spiritual fruit. *Without faith, spiritually fruitful living is impossible.*

Abraham—the father of our faith—believed God amid seemingly impossible circumstances. How are we doing as his spiritual children? When finances are thin, or circumstances bleak, or relationships strained, do we trust our Lord and Savior? Do we believe that He will meet our needs or guide us to favorable outcomes? I cannot speak for you, but I can attest to myself. I still have some growing to do!

A COVENANT WITH GOD ALMIGHTY!

After Abraham believed God, the Lord used a covenant introduction in proclaiming yet another interesting promise: "I am the Lord who brought you out of Ur of the Chaldeans, to give you this land to possess it" (Genesis 15:7). For his part, Abraham responded to God's promise with another question: "O Lord God, how may I know that I will possess it?"

We should not overlook the nuance in the man's response. People tend to question God in one of two ways. Some question with an attitude of skepticism and unbelief; others from a foundation of trust in a quest to understand. The former approach usually creates more doubts, while the latter releases a stream of life-giving grace.

We just saw that Abraham believed God, so his question was not an expression of doubt. Why did he ask it then? I believe that Abraham recognized God's covenantal language and thought, "Am I hearing what I think I am hearing?" Intrigued by what was happening, he asked the question in an attempt to get the Lord to reveal more of His plan. In response, the Almighty said something unthinkable that surely must have made Abraham's heart leap. He told the man to gather sacrificial animals for a covenant ceremony:

> Now when the sun was going down, a deep sleep fell upon Abram; and behold, terror and great darkness fell upon him. God said to Abram, "Know for certain that your descendants will be strangers in a land that is not theirs, where they will be enslaved and oppressed four hundred years. But I will also judge the nation whom they will serve, and afterward they will come out with many possessions. As for you, you shall go to your fathers in peace; you will be buried at a good old age. Then in the fourth generation they will return here, for the iniquity of the Amorite is not yet complete."
>
> It came about when the sun had set, that it was very dark, and behold, there appeared a smoking oven and a flaming torch which passed between these pieces. On that day the Lord made a covenant with Abram, saying,
>
> "To your descendants I have given this land,
> From the river of Egypt as far as the great river, the river Euphrates." Genesis 15:12–18

What role did Abraham play in establishing the covenant? He believed God. Then, in obedience, he gathered, sacrificed, and watched over the animals. After that, the mighty patriarch *fell asleep*. I can relate! More than once, I have dozed off during my own devotional times.

The problem with a covenant between God and humanity is that humans can never live up to their part of the deal. Think about Adam and Eve. The Lord gave them only one command, and yet they failed to keep even that. This covenant with Abraham was different. The Lord took upon Himself the weight of ratification, including the consequences of failing to uphold the covenant. God's covenant-friend Abraham simply received the promise by faith. It would be many years before the promise came to full fruition, but the pattern for divine-human interaction had been established. God carries the weight of the burden, and we trust Him to be faithful.

ISHMAEL

Faith is not a wishful belief lasting for a brief moment, but rather ongoing confidence that stands the test of time. Furthermore, our interaction with God goes "from faith to faith" (see Romans 1:1-17). Abraham and his wife Sarah began with a measure of faith and ended with a greater measure. The journey in between had plenty of peaks and valleys.

Genesis 16 records the birth of Ishmael. Sarah, being well past her childbearing years, was having serious doubts about God's promise. As a result, she convinced her husband to adopt a pagan custom by fathering a child through her maid—Hagar. The little boy, named Ishmael, later became the patriarch of the Arab nations.

The attempt to substitute a human solution for a divine promise is common to our race. Rarely do such efforts end well. With Abraham and Sarah, trying to fulfill God's promise according to their own wisdom planted the seeds for the centuries-long mess that we call the "Middle East conflict."

We cannot begin to measure how much pain has resulted from Abraham and Sarah's lapse. Even so, the New Testament writers make no mention of it. The God who is able to remember everything chose to remember nothing of His covenant-friends' failures. Here again, we catch a glimpse of the Lord's new covenant promises (Jeremiah 31:31-34; Hebrews 8:7-13). *At any given time, God could find a multitude of things wrong with each of our lives, but He chooses not to hold them against His covenant children.* From the moment of humanity's Edenic crash, the Lord has wanted to forgive our iniquities.

FRUITFULNESS RESTORED

Abraham was about seventy-five years old when the Lord first promised that he would become the father of a multitude. The aging patriarch did not father Ishmael until he was eighty-six, and it would be another fourteen years before he and Sarah bore a child together.

> Now when Abram was ninety-nine years old, the Lord appeared to Abram and said to him,
>
> "I am God Almighty;
> Walk before Me, and be blameless.
> I will establish My covenant between Me and you,
> And I will multiply you exceedingly."
>
> Abram fell on his face, and God talked with him, saying,
>
> "As for Me, behold, My covenant is with you,
> And you will be the father of a multitude of nations.
> No longer shall your name be called Abram,
> But your name shall be Abraham;
> For I have made you the father of a multitude of nations.
>
> I will make you exceedingly fruitful, and I will make nations of you, and kings will come forth from you. I will establish My covenant between Me and you and your descendants after you throughout their generations for an everlasting covenant, to be God to you and to your descendants after you." Genesis 17:1–7

For twenty-four long years, Abraham walked with God, his life defined by divine promises yet unfulfilled. The natural impossibility of his situation did not change, but during that season of seemingly unanswered prayer, his faith grew stronger and stronger (Romans 4:13–22).

In light of all that transpired in the garden of Eden, the Lord's promise to make Abraham exceedingly fruitful was massive! By all natural appearances, Abraham had been saddled with the curse of unfruitfulness, but God promised to bless him beyond measure. And because Abraham is the father of our faith, that promise is not limited to a lone individual who walked this planet thousands of years ago. Those who follow in the steps of Abraham's faith will bear their own rich measure of fruit.

NEW IDENTITIES

During this interaction, the Lord also gave the aged couple new identities. *Abram* (exalted father) became *Abraham* (the father of a multitude), and *Sarai* became *Sarah*. The variation in Sarah's name is slight; both names mean "princess." In a sense, God also gave *Himself* a new identity as He became "the God of Abraham." Later, as the lineage grew, it became "the God of Abraham, Isaac, and Jacob." Indeed, this is one of the names the Lord gave to Moses when they met at the burning bush about four hundred years later (Exodus 3:13–15). That the holy Creator of our massive cosmos would begin to define Himself through His relationship with a lineage of sinful humans is beyond comprehension!

Still, the ancient blood covenant forged between God and Abraham was not yet complete. At that time, the Lord required a bloody covenant sign (i.e., memorial) from Abraham. He and all the males of his household needed to be circumcised as a means to set them apart from all the other peoples of the earth. Ouch! The rich blessings of a covenant with God always exact a price, albeit one that pales in comparison to the blessings received.

A short time later, three representatives from God met Abraham at his tent and reminded him that Sarah would bear a son a year later. The Lord also made Abraham privy to His plans to destroy Sodom and Gomorrah for their extreme wickedness.

Abraham's response forever defines those who become his new covenant descendants through faith in Christ: he stepped in as a *mediator* between God and man. With Abraham as mediator, God declared that only reluctantly would He wield the sword of judgment over a people whose wickedness grieved the throne room of heaven. In the end, only Abraham's nephew Lot and his family were spared, but this unlikely dialogue between God and man makes a bold proclamation: *the heavenly Father allows the privileged status of His covenant children to influence His dealings with those outside the covenant.* Christians who grasp this reality are well on their way to understanding the concept of *intercessory prayer.*

Just as God had promised, Sarah conceived and bore Abraham a son (Isaac) the following year. It took twenty-five years for the promise to be fulfilled, but the Lord stood faithful to His word. Time does not mean to heaven what it means to earth.

GOD'S OATH

This part of our story concludes with God calling Abraham to offer his promised son as a human sacrifice. Abraham obeyed without hesitation and took Isaac to the place designated by the Lord. The aged man built an altar and covered it with wood for a fire. He then tied up Isaac and laid him on the wood, raising a knife into the air for a fatal blow.

What went through Abraham's mind at this time? We cannot know exactly, but he was on the verge of killing his promised and beloved son. Unlike an unstable parent who slays a child, Abraham knew God's voice intimately by this point in their relationship. And though the command to slay his son made no sense, the father of our faith gave no room for doubt. The Almighty God had been faithful to bring Abraham and his family to this point, and He would be faithful to make Isaac a multitude—even if it meant resurrecting the young lad from the dead.

Through an angel, the Lord stopped Abraham before the knife could fall. He only wanted to test the man's willingness to honor his covenant-Friend above his much-desired son.

But the angel of the Lord called to him from heaven and said, "Abraham, Abraham!" And he said, "Here I am." He said, "Do

> not stretch out your hand against the lad, and do nothing to him; for now I know that you fear God, since you have not withheld your son, your only son, from Me." Then Abraham raised his eyes and looked, and behold, behind him a ram caught in the thicket by his horns; and Abraham went and took the ram and offered him up for a burnt offering in the place of his son. Abraham called the name of that place The Lord Will Provide, as it is said to this day, "In the mount of the Lord it will be provided." Genesis 22:11–14

The mount where the Lord provided later became home to the Jewish temple; it is also near where Jesus gave His life as the sacrificial Lamb of God. Long before humanity understood the depth of its need, our covenant-keeping God had our provision in mind. Still, there is more:

> Then the angel of the Lord called to Abraham a second time from heaven, and said, "By Myself I have sworn, declares the Lord, because you have done this thing and have not withheld your son, your only son, indeed I will greatly bless you, and I will greatly multiply your seed as the stars of the heavens and as the sand which is on the seashore; and your seed shall possess the gate of their enemies. In your seed all the nations of the earth shall be blessed, because you have obeyed My voice." Genesis 22:15–18

Boom! What a powerful passage! Because Abraham believed God, he also obeyed Him in the most extreme circumstances. His was no shallow mental affirmation, but rather a substantive faith that led to obedience. God then swore a three-fold oath. This oath continues a powerful reversal of the Adamic curse, disarming Satan's power.

As already presented in God's promise of fruitfulness, the Lord will surely bless and multiply Abraham's seed. But there is more to the promise; Abraham's descendants will also possess the gates of their enemies. The nation of Israel knew this promise well, refusing to yield even under the oppressive thumbs of more powerful nations.

Under the new covenant, this promise of preeminence takes on a spiritual dynamic, applying to all Christians—including the Arabic descendants of Ishmael who embrace Jesus Christ as Lord and Savior. When we become Christians, by default, we enlist in a life-and-death war against the kingdom of darkness. God's oath to Abraham means that we are on the winning side:

> I also say to you that you are Peter [a stone], and upon this rock [bedrock] I will build My church; and the gates of Hades will not overpower it." Matthew 16:18

> The seventy returned with joy, saying, "Lord, even the demons are subject to us in Your name." And He said to them, "I was watching Satan fall from heaven like lightning. Behold, I have given you authority to tread on serpents and scorpions, and over all the power of the enemy, and nothing will injure you." Luke 10:17-19

The battle can feel overwhelming at times, but God's oath is sure. We *will* overcome the strongholds of spiritual darkness in this world so that the captives we love can be freed from the dominion of evil.

Finally, God's promise to Abraham ends where it began in Genesis 12:1-3. All the nations of the earth will taste the blessings of Abraham's faithful obedience. From our envious vantage point, we can see the fulfillment of this promise happening step by step. Areas of the world that were once dark with ignorance and spiritual poverty have been brought alive through the gospel of Jesus Christ. Much more remains to be done, but the Lord has sworn an oath, and as Abraham's spiritual descendants, we are given the privileged opportunity to play a part in His master plan.

WRAP-UP

The pattern of Abraham's story is repeated again and again in the lives of God's covenant children. We are all called to take risks by stepping out of the familiarity of our comfort zones and into unknown territory. It is a journey that takes us beyond our own small worlds and into an intimate and abiding relationship with the King of Glory. The God who created our cosmos no longer treats us as distant parties, but instead fully embraces us as His close covenant-friends.

We often struggle with areas of our lives where we feel "barren" and "childless," and our promised destiny feels painfully distant at times. But Abraham's story also encourages us to take heart and trust God, knowing full well that He ever seeks to bless the children He so dearly loves. The key is for us to trust Him and live by faith, no matter how bleak our circumstances might appear on the surface.

God's blessings, we must remember, are not just about us. We experience our fullest blessings only as we bless others, and one of the most powerful ways we can do that is by using our privileged status as the Lord's covenant-friends to "stand in the gap" as mediators for those who do not yet know Him. What an exciting and amazing privilege it is to influence the eternal destinies of others through prayer!

DISCUSSION

1. How does the pattern of Abraham's life affect Christians in our day?
2. How might this world change if Christians discover that their greatness is one of God's primary concerns?
3. The Lord told His covenant-friend Abraham that He would curse those who dishonored him (Genesis 12:3). What are the ramifications for those who mistreat Christians?
4. Please read Genesis 15:6 and Habakkuk 2:4. How do these verses relate to one another, and why are they significant?
5. How might the close relationship that Christians have with God provide hope for an unbeliever?
6. How do Matthew 16:13–18 and Luke 10:17–19 relate to God's oath in Genesis 22:15–18?

Chapter Five

THE MOSAIC AND DAVIDIC COVENANTS

Therefore the Law has become our tutor to lead us to Christ, so that we may be justified by faith.

Galatians 3:24

Christian holiness is not a matter of painstaking conformity to the individual precepts of an external law code; it is rather a question of the Holy Spirit's producing His fruit in the life, reproducing those graces which were seen in perfection in the life of Christ.

—F. F. Bruce

Loved, hated, blessed, persecuted, oppressed, prosperous, seemingly always at the center of controversy. If there is one group of people that would be considered puzzling in our world, it is the Jews. Their story is vital to the greatest story of all: God's covenant relationship with the human race. Following the many highs and lows of the Jewish experience recorded in the Bible leads us to the person of Jesus Christ.

The rich legacy of the Jews (Hebrews) began with Abraham and his wife Sarah—two people who trusted the Lord and His promises against seemingly impossible odds. By faith, these special friends of God gave birth to a son—Isaac—in their old age.

In turn, Isaac and his wife Rebekah brought a set of twins—Esau and Jacob—into this world. Esau, a hairy outdoorsman, was the older brother, and the rights of the firstborn son belonged to him. However, through a drama worthy of a modern soap opera, Esau despised his birthright and provided the much-weaker Jacob with an opportunity to steal the coveted blessing of the firstborn.

Unlike his grandfather Abraham, Jacob was not a faith-filled man of esteemed character. Nevertheless, he was God's chosen heir. Jacob's life is a testimony to the fact that the King of Glory can accomplish great things through seriously flawed people. *Greatness is not about human ability, but rather a divine investment in weak and broken vessels.* Through unlikely circumstances and almost innumerable human failures, the Creator of all things worked out a marvelous plan.

DRAMA

Wherever Jacob went, drama followed. This grandson of Abraham fell in love with his cousin Rachel, but through some trickery of his own, Uncle Laban instead gave him the unattractive Leah. Jacob then took Rachel as his second wife, setting the stage for decades of competition, chaos, and intrigue.

The two sisters competed continually against one another—a conflict exacerbated by Rachel's early barrenness. Rachel eventually gave birth to Joseph and Benjamin—Jacob's two favorites. Between Rachel, Leah, and their two maids, Jacob fathered twelve sons and at least one daughter.

A critical moment came when Jacob was fleeing his uncle's household with a large entourage of family and livestock. He had journeyed to Laban's alone and empty-handed, resting his head on rocks at night instead of pillows. Now, bursting with blessings, Jacob felt compelled to return to his homeland. At the same time, he was terrified at the thought of meeting Esau—the rougher older brother whose murderous threats had caused the conspirator to flee many years prior. God met Jacob before he encountered Esau and his men:

THE MOSAIC AND DAVIDIC COVENANTS 91

> Then Jacob was left alone, and a man wrestled with him until daybreak. When he saw that he had not prevailed against him, he touched the socket of his thigh; so the socket of Jacob's thigh was dislocated while he wrestled with him. Then he said, "Let me go, for the dawn is breaking." But he said, "I will not let you go unless you bless me." So he said to him, "What is your name?" And he said, "Jacob." He said, "Your name shall no longer be Jacob, but Israel; for you have striven with God and with men and have prevailed." . . . And he blessed him there. Genesis 32:24-29

Jacob was given the new name of *Israel*, which means "he contends with God."[1] In spite of his many shortcomings, Jacob had the tenacity to lay hold of the Lord and not let go. Almighty God was pleased, and a new identity was birthed.

We could say much more about Jacob and his family, but most of it lies outside the context of this study. Toward the end of his life, favored and overflowing with abundance, Jacob lived with honor in the land of Egypt. No longer alone, his clan now consisted of seventy family members. That number increased exponentially, but so did the hardship predicted by God.

At the appropriate time, the Lord's word spoken to Abraham (as recorded in Genesis 15:13-14) came to pass:

> Joseph [Jacob's son] died, and all his brothers and all that generation. But the sons of Israel were fruitful and increased greatly, and multiplied, and became exceedingly mighty, so that the land was filled with them.

> Now a new king arose over Egypt, who did not know Joseph. He said to his people, "Behold, the people of the sons of Israel are more and mightier than we. Come, let us deal wisely with them, or else they will multiply and in the event of war,

---

1. J. Barton Payne, "2287 שָׂרָה," ed. R. Laird Harris, Gleason L. Archer Jr., and Bruce K. Waltke, *Theological Wordbook of the Old Testament* (Chicago: Moody Press, 1999), 883.

they will also join themselves to those who hate us, and fight against us and depart from the land." So they appointed taskmasters over them to afflict them with hard labor. And they built for Pharaoh storage cities, Pithom and Raamses. But the more they afflicted them, the more they multiplied and the more they spread out, so that they were in dread of the sons of Israel. Exodus 1:6–12

THE MOSAIC COVENANT

Attempting to eradicate Hebrew power, the Egyptian Pharaoh resorted to infanticide. He ordered the death of all newborn males, but a woman named Jochebed could not bring herself to murder her son. She put him in a basket and floated it on the Nile River, while the infant's sister watched from afar. Pharaoh's daughter happened to see the baby and, having compassion, took him into her family. For forty years, Moses lived as a member of the Egyptian royal household—the most powerful and esteemed family in the known world. But even the fame and treasures of Egypt could not eradicate his Hebrew roots.

One day, Moses saw an Egyptian guard beating a Hebrew slave, and so he killed the guard, assuming that his fellow Hebrews understood that God was granting them deliverance through him (see Acts 7:20–25). The plan went awry, and Moses spent the next *forty years* of his life as a "stinking shepherd" (Genesis 46:34 tells us that the Egyptians despised shepherds) in a desolate wilderness.

When Moses was eighty years old, he had a life-changing encounter with God at a burning bush:

> Now Moses was pasturing the flock of Jethro his father-in-law, the priest of Midian; and he led the flock to the west side of the wilderness and came to Horeb, the mountain of God. The angel of the Lord appeared to him in a blazing fire from the midst of a bush; and he looked, and behold, the bush was burning with fire, yet the bush was not consumed. So Moses said, "I must turn aside now and see this marvelous sight,

why the bush is not burned up." When the Lord saw that he turned aside to look, God called to him from the midst of the bush and said, "Moses, Moses!" And he said, "Here I am." Then He said, "Do not come near here; remove your sandals from your feet, for the place on which you are standing is holy ground." He said also, "I am the God of your father, the God of Abraham, the God of Isaac, and the God of Jacob." Then Moses hid his face, for he was afraid to look at God.

The Lord said, "I have surely seen the affliction of My people who are in Egypt, and have given heed to their cry because of their taskmasters, for I am aware of their sufferings. So I have come down to deliver them from the power of the Egyptians, and to bring them up from that land to a good and spacious land, to a land flowing with milk and honey, to the place of the Canaanite and the Hittite and the Amorite and the Perizzite and the Hivite and the Jebusite. Now, behold, the cry of the sons of Israel has come to Me; furthermore, I have seen the oppression with which the Egyptians are oppressing them." Exodus 3:1–9

Notice that the Lord introduced Himself as "the God of Abraham, the God of Isaac, and the God of Jacob," and also referred to the Israelites as "My people." The passing of four hundred years had done nothing to weaken the strength of the covenant between God and Abraham. Furthermore, He had heard the cry of Israel and promised to deliver them from Egypt. A covenant promise given to Abraham was also reiterated; Canaan would be theirs.

Moses' intrigue quickly turned to trepidation as the Lord announced that He was going to use the aged man to deliver Israel from the mighty kingdom of Egypt. It would be like the coach of an American football team announcing a player as his new starting quarterback for the Super Bowl decades after that guy had retired. The aged shepherd's entire life, it turns out, had been a training ground to prepare him for this monumental task. But Moses could not see it, and so he balked at God's good plan:

> Then Moses said to the Lord, "Please, Lord, I have never been eloquent, neither recently nor in time past, nor since You have spoken to Your servant; for I am slow of speech and slow of tongue." The Lord said to him, "Who has made man's mouth? Or who makes him mute or deaf, or seeing or blind? Is it not I, the Lord? Now then go, and I, even I, will be with your mouth, and teach you what you are to say." But he said, "Please, Lord, now send the message by whomever You will."
>
> Then the anger of the Lord burned against Moses, and He said, "Is there not your brother Aaron the Levite? I know that he speaks fluently. And moreover, behold, he is coming out to meet you; when he sees you, he will be glad in his heart. You are to speak to him and put the words in his mouth; and I, even I, will be with your mouth and his mouth, and I will teach you what you are to do." Exodus 4:10–15

Here was an eighty-year-old man, beaten down by the circumstances of life, being called by God for a dynamic purpose. It would be an understatement to say that Moses felt inadequate. His experience at the burning bush sends a powerful message to all of us. No matter how ill-equipped we might feel to accomplish what God has called us to do, we do not have the right to refuse Him. Our Creator always knows what He is doing, and He is in the habit of choosing unlikely people for significant tasks. *God became angry with Moses only when the man proclaimed his inadequacies to be larger than the Lord's sufficiency.* Fear, it seems, makes a poor excuse for refusing to obey God.

    Debi and I are not risk-takers by nature, but many years ago, the Lord called me to leave the apparent security of a career in analytical chemistry. The salary and benefits had been excellent, but we knew that my path led in a different direction. Added to the challenge of an uncertain salary, I found myself, time after time, doing tasks for which I felt ill-equipped. Nobody had taught me how to start a nonprofit organization or a publishing ministry—or how to write a book, for that matter. Having wrestled with feelings of inadequacy more times than I can count, I certainly understand Moses' struggle.

THE MOSAIC AND DAVIDIC COVENANTS

If a person's life purpose is from God, you can be sure that it will involve considerable discomfort. However haltingly, we must move forward in obedience to our Maker's calling. As both Abraham and Moses took risks and stepped out of their comfort zones, the covenant-keeping God promised that He would be with them every step of the way. And He was! *The Lord's covenant promises are no less viable to us today.*

The Exodus

Through the story of the exodus, yet another amazing drama unfolded. After a series of ten miraculous plagues, the Lord delivered the people of Israel from Egypt in a rush of glory. This deliverance story paints yet another insightful picture of our new covenant reality. Pharaoh represents Satan, who keeps God's people enslaved and oppressed. Moses, meanwhile, represents Jesus as he brings about a mighty deliverance from slavery and oppression. The Lord empowered Israel to defeat a host of wicked nations so that they could take dominion of the "Promised Land"—a fruitful territory flowing with milk and honey. The Promised Land does not represent heaven (we will have no enemies there), but rather symbolizes the overcoming, fruitful life of a Christian.

The last of the ten plagues killed every one of Egypt's firstborn males, but God spared His covenant people through the blood of the sacrificial Passover lamb. The imagery of the Passover story shines a spotlight toward the sacrificial death and resurrection of Jesus, which took place over a thousand years later.

Not long after their dramatic deliverance from Egypt, the Lord spoke to Moses on Mt. Sinai:

> Moses went up to God, and the Lord called to him from the mountain, saying, "Thus you shall say to the house of Jacob and tell the sons of Israel: 'You yourselves have seen what I did to the Egyptians, and how I bore you on eagles' wings, and brought you to Myself. Now then, if you will indeed

> obey My voice and keep My covenant, then you shall be My own possession among all the peoples, for all the earth is Mine; and you shall be to Me a kingdom of priests and a holy nation.' These are the words that you shall speak to the sons of Israel."
>
> So Moses came and called the elders of the people, and set before them all these words which the Lord had commanded him. All the people answered together and said, "All that the Lord has spoken we will do!" And Moses brought back the words of the people to the Lord. Exodus 19:3-8

At this moment, the Creator of our vast cosmos initiated a covenant with Abraham's descendants. The pact with Abraham was no less applicable, but through this "Mosaic covenant," God would accomplish a special purpose by establishing a nation and its system of laws.

Enthusiasm ran high that day as the people realized their special status in the eyes of Almighty God. The story of their father Abraham, it turned out, was no mere fable. Excited and naive, the people shouted, "All that the Lord has spoken, we will do!"—before they even knew the full terms of the covenant.

A Divine Visitation

God went on to tell the people to prepare for a divine visitation by washing their garments and abstaining from sex for three days. Shortly after that, the massive family group of newly liberated slaves had a close encounter of the divine kind:

> So it came about on the third day, when it was morning, that there were thunder and lightning flashes and a thick cloud upon the mountain and a very loud trumpet sound, so that all the people who were in the camp trembled. And Moses brought the people out of the camp to meet God, and they stood at the foot of the mountain. Exodus 19:16-17

THE MOSAIC AND DAVIDIC COVENANTS

> All the people perceived the thunder and the lightning flashes and the sound of the trumpet and the mountain smoking; and when the people saw it, they trembled and stood at a distance. Then they said to Moses, "Speak to us yourself and we will listen; but let not God speak to us, or we will die." Moses said to the people, "Do not be afraid; for God has come in order to test you, and in order that the fear of Him may remain with you, so that you may not sin." So the people stood at a distance, while Moses approached the thick cloud where God was. Exodus 20:18–21

God warned the people to stay at a safe distance, but they took things even further; Moses would buffer the intensity of God's glory. The Creator of all things was coming to dwell in their midst, but the people were so afraid that they wanted to know Him only from afar.

I cannot begin to imagine the overwhelming nature of this experience. Just a tiny display of the Almighty's power is enough to knock the stoutest person off-kilter. Coming into God's unfiltered presence is an unsettling experience—especially for the sinful, naked soul. It is a place where even the most pious people are undone.

Imagine standing naked in a stadium filled with 100,000 perfect people. As you stand there shaking, the focus of undivided attention, a huge billboard begins to display every self-centered action, unkind word, and bad thought you have ever had. Naked and fully exposed before 200,000 piercing eyes, you have nowhere to go. Add a nonstop earthquake and a few hundred lightning flashes to the mix, and you might have a small taste of what it would be like to stand before God's throne without being cleansed of your sins (see also Isaiah 6:1–5).

As part of the encounter with Moses and the people of Israel, the Lord also gave the *Ten Commandments* (aka the Decalogue)—a list of covenant stipulations that would form the foundation of "the Mosaic law" (Exodus 20:1–17). After hearing the Ten Commandments, along with many other requirements for righteous living, the people again proclaimed their confidence to obey:

> Then Moses came and recounted to the people all the words of the Lord and all the ordinances; and all the people answered with one voice and said, "All the words which the Lord has spoken we will do!" Exodus 24:3

> Then he took the book of the covenant and read it in the hearing of the people; and they said, "All that the Lord has spoken we will do, and we will be obedient!" Exodus 24:7

Moses and the Jewish elders then went before the presence of God and shared a covenant meal (Exodus 24:9-11). Soon after, the Lord called Moses and his assistant Joshua back up to Mt. Sinai.

By the time that Moses and Joshua came back down from the mountain with the two stone tablets of the Decalogue, the Israelites had already broken the first two commandments by fashioning a golden calf (an idol) to be their god (Exodus 32). Three thousand men died as a result of that transgression. Many more would descend to their graves in the chaotic years that followed.

At their core, the Ten Commandments focused on loving God and loving others. When the people of Israel met those standards of love, they were declared to be *righteous*—approved and in right standing with their holy Creator. When they failed to meet those standards, they were given the opportunity to cleanse their guilt with an elaborate system of sacrifices. Regardless of the many rituals and requirements, the heart of the Mosaic law was always to be about love (Deuteronomy 30:11-16; Matthew 22:34-40). Sadly, for many ancient Jews, their focus centered on rules rather than relationships.

God's Presence

Among other instructions for ceremonial and religious ritual, the Lord included the design of the *tabernacle*—a portable tent in which He would dwell as He traveled with the people of Israel. *The Creator of billions of galaxies chose to set up house among a group of former slaves on a tiny planet called "Earth."*

THE MOSAIC AND DAVIDIC COVENANTS

God's nearness to humanity presents yet another challenging concept. If our Creator is everywhere, how can we not be near to Him? The paradox is that we can be both near the Lord and far from Him at the same time. Because of the Edenic crash, our innate sinfulness has rendered all humans "dead" to God. Furthermore, our natural eyes are blind to the Lord's spiritual presence. In his message on Mars Hill in Athens, the apostle Paul said:

> "The God who made the world and all things in it, since He is Lord of heaven and earth, does not dwell in temples made with hands; nor is He served by human hands, as though He needed anything, since He Himself gives to all people life and breath and all things; and He made from one man every nation of mankind to live on all the face of the earth, having determined their appointed times and the boundaries of their habitation, that they would seek God, if perhaps they might grope for Him and find Him, though He is not far from each one of us; for in Him we live and move and exist." Acts 17:24–28a

According to the Scriptures, we have the ability to "find" the Lord's presence in three distinct ways. First, we need to understand that our Creator is *omnipresent*. God is everywhere, and there is nowhere that He is not (Psalm 139:7–12). There are also times when the *manifest presence* of the Lord touches our physical senses. When the tabernacle was consecrated, for example, the "*Shekinah* glory cloud" of God was so thick that Moses could not even enter in (Exodus 40:34–35). On another occasion, the priests could not stand in His presence (1 Kings 8:10–11). Finally, and perhaps most importantly for us, we can speak of the *indwelling presence* of God, which mysteriously takes up residence in the hearts of His covenant people (Acts 2:1–21).

Under the Mosaic covenant, God's presence dwelt in the *Holy of Holies*—a special room within the tabernacle the people of Israel carried from place to place as they journeyed through the wilderness. Later, they built a more permanent structure, but the basic design remained the same. The Lord dwelt in the midst of His people, but they were still separated from Him by the walls of the tabernacle and by a thick curtain (veil) that hung from ceiling to floor.

The Mosaic covenant provided people with an opportunity to relate to God from a distance through a combination of self-effort, various offerings, and a system of blood sacrifices. But apart from Moses and Joshua, the only individuals permitted to access God's presence were the Levitical priests—an elite group of men who were trained and set apart for that intent. Like Abraham, those priests served as mediators between God and humanity.

Later, when Jesus died on the cross, a supernatural Power tore the temple veil in two pieces, forever ending the separation between God and His people (Matthew 27:50-51). Under the new covenant, *God's covenant children* are cleansed by the blood of Jesus to become the "Holy of Holies" in which His presence dwells.

With the new covenant, there is no wall, no veil, no distance. All Christians are "mini-temples" in which the presence of God dwells. *Everything about Christianity is designed for us to draw near to our heavenly Father.* The idea of serving the Lord from a distance might still be common in our day, but it is not Christian.

Law

The Ten Commandments were written on tablets of cold, hard, unyielding stone. The nature of that stone reflects the state of human hearts since the day Adam and Eve ate from the tree of the knowledge of good and evil. In every culture, hardened hearts naturally look down with judgment and contempt upon those who fail to meet their standards of *cultural righteousness.*

In total, the Mosaic law provided 613 moral, civil, and ceremonial standards that the people were required to meet if they wanted to be approved as righteous before God. Human imperfection was accounted for with a system of blood sacrifices. Still, law breeds judgment, and so God's dealings with humanity—His people

THE MOSAIC AND DAVIDIC COVENANTS

included—changed dramatically after the law was given. Before the giving of the law, there were only a couple of extreme cases (Noah's flood and the destruction of Sodom and Gomorrah) when the Lord poured out wrath upon humanity. After the giving of the Mosaic law, however, virtually every act of unbelief or rebellion was met with a torrent of judgment.

Reading the stories of God's dealings with ancient Israel, we are likely to be repulsed by the harsh judgment meted out on a seemingly routine basis. We should be! At the same time, we should also remember that the Mosaic law does not reflect God's heart. Through that religious system, the Lord dealt with humanity according to our natural law-based mindset that finds its roots in the tree of the knowledge of good and evil. If He had been pleased with the old covenant, there would have been no need for the blood of Jesus to be spilled to establish another. All along, our merciful God sought to steer the human race toward His new covenant paradigm of grace.

We can identify the primary purpose of the law through a self-confident statement thrice repeated by the people of Israel: "All that the Lord has spoken we will do!" (Exodus 19:8; 24:3, 7). This statement related to the many requirements of the Mosaic law, which released rich blessings for obedience, but terrible curses for disobedience (see Deuteronomy 27–29).

> For all who rely on works of the law are under a curse;
> for it is written, "Cursed be everyone who does not abide
> by all things written in the Book of the Law, and do them."
> Galatians 3:10 (ESV)

The purpose of the law is profound! There is something within humanity that innately desires to conform to God's goodness. For example, we have all experienced the common grace of feeling good when we help others in need. The problem, though, is that our law-based mentality leads to *self-exaltation*, and we soon begin to laud ourselves for our goodness. The overall standard, however, is one of *perfection*. But rather than providing us with the means to climb a "stairway to heaven," the harsh requirements of the law expose our *inability* to achieve divine perfection.

Our race needed to learn the pain-ridden lesson that we cannot meet God's standards of flawless love and moral purity through self-effort. Thus, the Mosaic covenant was not an end within itself, but rather a "stepping stone" to a far better covenant. The law served its purpose by enslaving self-confident humanity to sin so that the Lord could mercifully bless all who believe through the promise of faith in Jesus Christ (Galatians 3:22).

THE DAVIDIC COVENANT

Reuben was Jacob's firstborn, and the Messianic lineage should have gone to him, but the young man slept with his father's concubine. The next two sons also committed serious transgressions. Judah—Jacob's fourth-born—was no saint, but the lineage went through him nonetheless. The story of Judah's birth provides an interesting perspective:

> Now the Lord saw that Leah was unloved, and He opened her womb, but Rachel was barren. Leah conceived and bore a son and named him Reuben, for she said, "Because the Lord has seen my affliction; surely now my husband will love me." Then she conceived again and bore a son and said, "Because the Lord has heard that I am unloved, He has therefore given me this son also." So she named him Simeon. She conceived again and bore a son and said, "Now this time my husband will become attached to me, because I have borne him three sons." Therefore he was named Levi. And she conceived again and bore a son and said, "This time I will praise the Lord." Therefore she named him Judah. Then she stopped bearing. Genesis 29:31–35

Through her first three sons, the insecure and unloved Leah looked for validation, but it never came. At the birth of Judah, however, she

THE MOSAIC AND DAVIDIC COVENANTS

had a moment of clarity. Instead of finding her importance through childbirth, Leah chose to praise the Lord for His goodness. The name Judah links closely to the Hebrew word for praise, which involves making a public declaration of God's attributes and works.[2] The royal line of Israel would descend through Judah. More importantly, it was the lineage through which Jesus the Messiah was destined to come.

Leah's reaction to Judah's birth aligns perfectly with the Lord's design for our human identity. Our significance is established not by our ability to measure up to a multitude of religious, moral, or cultural standards (such as having male children), but through a covenant relationship with the King of Glory. He alone is our significance and the source of a secure identity.

Later, the Lord made a special covenant promise to one of Judah's descendants—King David. David was a former shepherd, considered by God to be a man after His own heart (Acts 13:22–23). The Lord's promise to the king once again points us toward Jesus Christ (see also Jeremiah 33:14–26):

> "When your days are complete and you lie down with your fathers, I will raise up your descendant after you, who will come forth from you, and I will establish his kingdom. He shall build a house for My name, and I will establish the throne of his kingdom forever. I will be a father to him and he will be a son to Me; when he commits iniquity, I will correct him with the rod of men and the strokes of the sons of men, but My lovingkindness shall not depart from him, as I took it away from Saul, whom I removed from before you. Your house and your kingdom shall endure before Me forever; your throne shall be established forever." 2 Samuel 7:12–16

Through God's interaction with David, we do not see the formal trappings of a covenant, but there is so much covenantal language

---

2. Ralph H. Alexander, "847 יָדָה," ed. R. Laird Harris, Gleason L. Archer Jr., and Bruce K. Waltke, *Theological Wordbook of the Old Testament* (Chicago: Moody Press, 1999), 365.

involved with this promise that the evidence of a covenant is difficult to deny. The physical throne of Israel did not endure, but David's house was forever established through the coming of Jesus—the eternal Son of God who also became *the Son of Man*. Of Him, we will have much more to say.

WRAP-UP

Like the ones that came before, the Mosaic and Davidic covenants served vital purposes in the progression of the Lord's relationship with humanity. Both point us toward Jesus, and through them we find powerful insights into the nature of the new and better covenant. And though our human existence is often characterized by issues of law and judgment, our God has been planning something far better since the dawn of time. Before moving onto the new covenant, however, we will wade into the waters of another Old Testament covenant that looms large in our Christian experience: the marriage covenant.

DISCUSSION

1. Why is someone so flawed as Jacob lauded as a hero of the faith (Hebrews 11:21)?
2. According to Exodus 4:10, what was the one thing that caused God to get angry with Moses?
3. How do you think Moses' experiences in the palace and as a shepherd would have prepared him for his role as the deliverer of Israel?
4. Please read Acts 17:24-28a. How can God be both near and far at the same time?
5. What was the primary purpose of the Mosaic law?
6. Please read 2 Samuel 7:12-16. How does the Davidic covenant find its fulfillment in Jesus?

PART III
THE MARRIAGE COVENANT

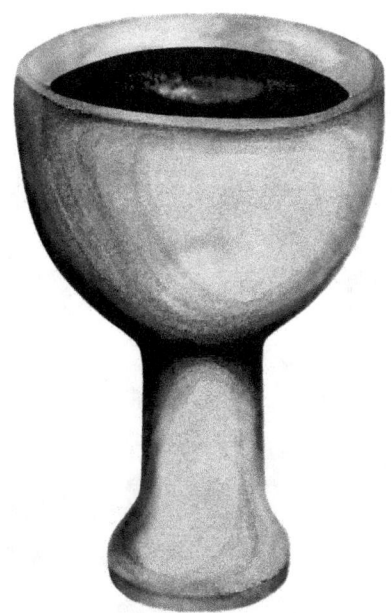

For this reason a man shall leave his father and his mother,
and be joined to his wife; and they shall become one flesh.
Genesis 2:24

Chapter Six

THE COVENANT FAMILY

For this reason a man shall leave his father and his mother, and be joined to his wife; and they shall become one flesh.

Genesis 2:24

There comes a point where we need to stop just pulling people out of the river. We need to go upstream and find out why they're falling in.

—Archbishop Desmond Tutu

With humidity nearing 100 percent, a hazy mist rose from the wet pavement. A heavy August downpour had done nothing to cool the air. Debi and I did not care. It was our wedding day! Filled with excitement and stress, much of the ceremony remains a blur in my mind. Of the memories that do stand out, one is a bit odd. Perhaps because it relates to a funny situation amid the wedding day stress.

The pastor officiating the ceremony, Ted, was on the way to becoming a close friend of ours. His daughter had been a college classmate, and we had been blessed by his messages at one of our campus ministry retreats. After several weekend visits to Ted and his wife Lou for premarital counseling, the day had finally arrived for Debi and me to exchange vows and rings.

Though the rented sanctuary was beautiful, air conditioning was not in the church's budget. Wearing his Methodist robe, the pastor suffered through the heat as much as the rest of us. Debi and I tried our best to focus on Ted's steady voice as he walked us through the ceremony, but an unexpected distraction kept grabbing our attention—the beads of sweat that were forming and gathering on Reverend Ted's balding head. Trickling down his face, some of them had combined to form a drop on the tip of his nose. Teetering between his eyes and his mouth, that mesmerizing drop demanded our focus as it grew larger and larger. I suppose that part of our fascination involved anticipating when the drop would fall onto the very formal notebook from which Ted was reading. Whether the drop fell or not, I really cannot remember; it is the image of it hanging there on the tip of the pastor's nose that lingers in my memory.

Many years have passed since that day. During that time, my wife and I have raised two children, enjoyed seasons of financial prosperity, and also struggled through times of need—a challenge that usually goes along with raising children. We have enjoyed good health, but also suffered under the burden of sickness. We have worked much too hard at times, while still enjoying the many blessings of family life. And we have both changed—in good ways, mostly. Most importantly, we did all of these things *together*, bound not by ever-changing feelings, but by an enduring covenant bond of love.

I cannot say that our marriage relationship has always been harmonious. Bringing two people of different genders, family backgrounds, and personalities together is bound to present its challenges, and not only for a season or two. Just when one spouse thinks he or she has the other one figured out . . . well, let me just say that even people we know intimately can surprise us.

Do I recommend marriage? Absolutely! But married life is not for the weak in spirit. Yes, Debi and I have known many couples who have enjoyed years of blessed wedlock, but also many others whose marriages did not weather the storms of life. This is one of the reasons that I find marriage to be the most difficult Biblical covenant to address. Making matters even more challenging, cultural shifts over the decades have created mass confusion regarding marriage and sexuality. Even devoted Christians sometimes disagree vehemently about the issues involved.

Each of the foundational covenants that we have addressed up to this point has a steady constant: God. In every pact, an all-wise, sovereign, loving, and faithful God was providing an unchangeable reality through which humanity's self-inflicted brokenness could be made whole. No matter what people did throughout Biblical history, there was always the constancy of a divine reality. The marriage covenant is different. Even though marriage is a sacred covenant ordained by God, it is a bond between two imperfect—and sometimes sin-infested—humans. And while this union has the potential for beauty and euphoria, it can also go badly—as it often does.

This line of thinking brings us to another major difficulty. Interrelated issues such as marriage, sexuality, and identity touch the most sensitive places in our lives. And while public—and political—issues such as these play out in the *macro* arenas of principles, policies, and laws, there is always a *micro* dynamic where vulnerable people get caught in the vortex between larger movements.

Certainly, Christians carry a mandate to stand for the integrity of Biblical truth, but love also cautions us not to trample vulnerable and hurting people under the wheels of public activism. This task is made especially challenging by a controversy-driven, social-media-steeped culture that seeks to shape public opinion through sound-bites and memes rather than by addressing difficult topics through thoughtful, meaningful, and gracious dialogue. Sometimes, the perceived failure of a Christian leader to publicly stand for righteousness has nothing to do with the fear of man; instead, it involves an intentional effort to avoid the fireworks of public drama for the sake of the vulnerable.

I appreciate the media of print because it allows me to choose my words carefully. No one is perfect, but I labor hard to grasp and communicate Biblical truths accurately. Teaching the truths of the Bible in love—yet without compromise—is always my goal because it is in drinking His truth that we find life. Those who drink truth are then able to live and speak truth. On the converse, straying from God's reality creates a slippery slope that can quickly propel us into a muck of damaged and broken relationships. The secret in all of this is to discover the Lord's good design and to align our lives accordingly.

OUR CREATOR'S DESIGN

We find God's design for marriage laid out in Genesis 1 and 2. Each chapter covers much of the same content from a slightly different perspective. For teaching purposes, I will combine two passages from these chapters, but in reversed order:

> Then the Lord God said, "It is not good for the man to be alone; I will make him a helper suitable for him." Out of the ground the Lord God formed every beast of the field and every bird of the sky, and brought them to the man to see what he would call them; and whatever the man called a living creature, that was its name. The man gave names to all the cattle, and to the birds of the sky, and to every beast of the field, but for Adam there was not found a helper suitable for him. So the Lord God caused a deep sleep to fall upon the man, and he slept; then He took one of his ribs and closed up the flesh at that place. The Lord God fashioned into a woman the rib which He had taken from the man, and brought her to the man. The man said,
>
> "This is now bone of my bones,
> And flesh of my flesh;
> She shall be called Woman,
> Because she was taken out of Man."
>
> For this reason a man shall leave his father and his mother, and be joined to his wife; and they shall become one flesh. And the man and his wife were both naked and were not ashamed. Genesis 2:18–25

God created man in His own image, in the image of God He created him; male and female He created them. God blessed them; and God said to them, "Be fruitful and multiply, and fill the earth, and subdue it; and rule over the fish of the sea and over the birds of the sky and over every living thing that moves on the earth." Then God said, "Behold, I have given you every plant yielding seed that is on the surface of all the earth, and every tree which has fruit yielding seed; it shall be food for you; and to every beast of the earth and to every bird of the sky and to every thing that moves on the earth which has life, I have given every green plant for food"; and it was so. God saw all that He had made, and behold, it was very good. Genesis 1:27–31a

These two passages are rich in theological truth and meaning! It was God who proclaimed man's need for companionship (Genesis 2:18). Paradise was not yet fully paradise, so the Lord created Eve as a helper for Adam while he slept. Eve was God's handiwork, made of the same basic "stuff" as Adam. Being neither lord nor slave, she was created from Adam's side—not from his head or his feet. Highly impressed, Adam recognized Eve to be of like kind and an extension of himself—and an appealing one at that!

The nature of the relationship between the first man and woman established a pattern designed to foster life in all its fullness. Having been created first, Adam was given a leadership role, but neither sex was intended to dominate the other.

Also, and of the utmost importance, it was God who established the marriage covenant. "For this reason a man shall leave his father and his mother, and be joined to his wife; and they shall become one flesh" (Genesis 2:24).

When the Lord finished His creative efforts, He looked at the summation of His work and saw that it was "very good" (Genesis 1:31). In God's own eyes, the design of His creation was exceedingly good. It is of that goodness that we all long to imbibe.

If we view this world as bad and full of dysfunction, we must remind ourselves of the contrast between our Creator's good design and the painful reality of the Adamic curse. The secret to life lies not in abandoning Biblical principles, but in aligning ourselves with His covenantal design. Someone with a tragic family history, for example, might embark on a personal crusade against the traditional family paradigm, but not only does this approach fail to heal past hurts, it also leads to the breaking of other lives.

The Lord's declaration of the two becoming one extends far beyond Adam and Eve; they were already of the same flesh and bone. It is here that we find our Creator's covenantal design for the human family, which is to be the building block for healthy societies. When a man and woman covenant together in marriage, they are to leave the authority of their parents to form a new family unit. Generation after generation, families keep societies cohesive.

God created humanity as male and female, and it is the unified relationship of the sexes that accurately reflects His image (Genesis 1:27). One gender is not better than the other. Instead, they differ uniquely, complementing one another in profound ways. This complimentary design is highlighted by the fact that Adam and Eve were both naked and yet unashamed (Genesis 2:25). In spite of their vulnerability, neither felt belittled or feared being exploited. Such marital bliss was to be the foundation upon which the human race would be fruitful and multiply. Is this not the very essence of paradise?

Marriage forms a solid foundation for the human family, which at its core, was designed to be a covenantal entity in which trust flourishes. Family terminology (e.g., brothers and sisters) is also used in the church—another key covenant community. The desire for tightly bound, faithful relationships is so universal that many close-knit, high-commitment groups such as military units, fraternities, sororities, sports teams, and even criminal organizations have chosen to adopt the language of family.

The concept of family, however, has been especially confused in recent years by popular media. Mainstream movies, sitcoms, and music rarely portray Biblical concepts accurately. A "family" is now characterized as virtually any close-knit group of people, such as coworkers, who spend a lot of time together for a common purpose. In these various groups, the "flavor" of family might be present, but the substance of covenant is not.

In the garden of Eden, God also made abundant provision for His human creatures, allowing Adam and Eve to eat freely from the abundant products of the ground. Only after the flood of Noah did the Lord give permission for humans to eat meat. Then, under the Mosaic law, He declared some animals to be unclean (not permissible for eating). Finally, through the new covenant, He proclaimed all animals to be clean. These changes were not arbitrary; they help illustrate covenant dynamics. Humanity's menu was established by its Creator, and each time God made an adjustment, He proclaimed the change in the context of another covenant. This is how divine covenants work—only the Lord has the authority to change the terms.

If human covenants are considered to be set in stone, how much more permanent is a covenant decreed by the Almighty God?

> Brethren, I speak in terms of human relations: even though it is only a man's covenant, yet when it has been ratified, no one sets it aside or adds conditions to it. Galatians 3:15

No man, woman, or government, no matter how wealthy, powerful, or influential, has the authority to alter what the Creator of our cosmos has established. *A covenant established by God is unalterable by humanity, and if He does change the terms of a covenant, He takes deliberate care to inform us of the change.* Of course, we can live as though God and His covenants are nonexistent, but somewhere down the road, our rebellion will exact a steep price.

FAITHFULNESS AND LOVINGKINDNESS

Being married to the same person for a very long time does not always feel good, and there will be times when abandoning a marriage covenant for other options seems desirable. The key, during these seasons, is to remember God's faithfulness toward us and to cultivate faithfulness in return. Remembering our vows—those supposedly unbreakable oaths made during a marriage covenant ceremony—is also vital. If I had some advice to give to a young pastor who officiates weddings, it would be to gift every newly married couple with a nicely designed copy of their wedding vows. In spite of wearing expensive rings as tokens of our faithfulness, our Western mindsets forget such weighty matters far too easily.

Marriage, however, is not just about cold, hard commitment. Nobody wants a miserable or abusive relationship. *If faithfulness is the bond that makes a marriage endure, lovingkindness is the element that makes it sweet.* By God's grace, a husband and wife learn to nurture a generous love toward each other by keeping the other person close at heart and expressing a kindness that lasts not just for weeks, months, or years, but a lifetime.

If we add a little—actually, a lot is necessary—wisdom to the mix, faithfulness and lovingkindness will produce a secure and fulfilling relationship that welcomes the richness of heaven to earth. And that is what marriage is *supposed* to do: provide a taste of our relationship with God.

> At the same time it must be borne in mind, that marriage conveyed to the Jews much higher thoughts than merely those of festivity and merriment. The pious fasted before it, confessing their sins. It was regarded almost as a Sacrament. Entrance into the marriage state was thought to carry the forgiveness of sins. It almost seems as if the relationships of Husband and Bride between Jehovah and His people, so frequently insisted upon, not only in the Bible, but in Rabbinic writings, had always been standing out [in] the background. Thus the bridal pair on the marriage-day symbolized the union of God and Israel.[1]

---

1. Alfred Edersheim, *The Life and Times of Jesus the Messiah* (Peabody, MA: Hendrickson Publishers, Inc., 1993), 244.

The Jews of Jesus' day held marriage ceremonies in such high regard that even funeral trains had to give way for a marriage procession.[2] The early Christian perspective of marriage did not exactly match the dynamics of the Jewish, but it was no less significant:

> Wives, be subject to your own husbands, as to the Lord. For the husband is the head of the wife, as Christ also is the head of the church, He Himself being the Savior of the body. But as the church is subject to Christ, so also the wives ought to be to their husbands in everything.
>
> Husbands, love your wives, just as Christ also loved the church and gave Himself up for her, so that He might sanctify her, having cleansed her by the washing of water with the word, that He might present to Himself the church in all her glory, having no spot or wrinkle or any such thing; but that she would be holy and blameless. So husbands ought also to love their own wives as their own bodies. He who loves his own wife loves himself; for no one ever hated his own flesh, but nourishes and cherishes it, just as Christ also does the church, because we are members of His body. For this reason a man shall leave his father and mother and shall be joined to his wife, and the two shall become one flesh. This mystery is great; but I am speaking with reference to Christ and the church. Ephesians 5:22–32

The marriage of a man and a woman, as close as it can come to the ideal, paints for us a picture of Jesus and His bride—the church. The marriage of a man and woman is sacred because it provides a visible image that profoundly reflects our relationship with the Lord. If we understand the dynamics of a faithful and loving marriage, we can better grasp the dynamics of the love relationship between Jesus and His church.

When a man and woman join together in a marriage covenant, they do so willingly. Giving their hearts fully to one another, each

---

2. Edersheim, *The Life and Times of Jesus the Messiah,* 244.

covenant party voluntarily restricts personal freedom for the sake of the other. Far more powerful than human-made rules, covenant love governs the dynamics of a marriage relationship—at least, that is the way God designed it to be.

And for those who bristle at the idea of a male taking the primary leadership role in the home, Paul is just reinforcing the dynamic that God established in Eden. Furthermore, a man who loves his wife as Christ loves the church would be a fantastic catch for any woman. Not to put any pressure on my married male readers, but something as simple as opening a door for your wife might unlock more than you realize!

CIRCUMCISION OF THE HEART

On the eighth day of his life, a Jewish male infant is circumcised. Many other cultures employ the same practice of cutting away the infant's foreskin, but for different reasons. In our modern world, circumcision is thought to bring better health. To the Jews, it means being faithful to the Abrahamic covenant (Genesis 17:9–14). Furthermore, this bloody ritual continues to be celebrated with a covenant meal, as in the days of old.

Just as with blood brotherhood rites and ceremonies, covenant circumcision can appear to be bizarre and senseless. But again, our examples from the Old Testament help illuminate the profound reality of the new covenant.

A sacred transfer of life takes place through the male sperm. Abraham's circumcision represented a cutting away of human sinfulness so that God-ordained life could be imparted. Circumcision also offered non-Jews the opportunity to join the covenant family of God. In the new covenant, circumcision takes on a spiritual meaning. *Human hearts*, not physical bodies, are circumcised. By hearts, we speak not of the physical organs, but the ethereal elements of mind, will, and emotion that control our behavior. Through the heart, spiritual life is imparted, and humans become fruitful. Both the Old and New Testaments refer to the unseen reality of a circumcised heart:

> "Moreover the Lord your God will circumcise your heart and the heart of your descendants, to love the Lord your God with all your heart and with all your soul, so that you may live." Deuteronomy 30:6

> For he is not a Jew who is one outwardly, nor is circumcision that which is outward in the flesh. But he is a Jew who is one inwardly; and circumcision is that which is of the heart, by the Spirit, not by the letter; and his praise is not from men, but from God. Romans 2:28–29

> And in Him you were also circumcised with a circumcision made without hands, in the removal of the body of the flesh by the circumcision of Christ; having been buried with Him in baptism, in which you were also raised up with Him through faith in the working of God, who raised Him from the dead. Colossians 2:11–12

But what does circumcision of the heart have to do with marriage? Jesus told the Jews that *hardened hearts* were at the root of their divorces (Matthew 19:8). In this regard, not much has changed in two thousand years.

Circumcision of the heart involves a cutting away of the core elements of human pride that harden our hearts: *self-centeredness*, *self-sovereignty* (i.e., the desire to be in control), and *self-glorification*. It is with circumcised hearts that the Lord calls us to approach both our understanding and our fulfillment of the marriage covenant.

- Cutting away self-centeredness: Many marriages struggle or fail because a spouse innately expects to be at the center of the household. But those who join with Christ through the new covenant yield centrality to God. Stepping out from a self-centered existence influences a relationship beyond measure.

- Cutting away self-sovereignty: Whether it be by physical intimidation or subtle cunning, controlling forces will also destroy the quality of our family relationships. As Christians, we surrender control to God, seeking to honor His will above our own. And when circumcised hearts yield to God's will, the blessings of His kingdom multiply within a household.

- Cutting away self-glorification: Just as Lucifer sought to rise to God's throne, so too, human pride seeks to glorify itself apart from God. This quest to find significance within ourselves—but through the approval of others—not only puts us at odds with the King of Glory, it also creates problems within our marriages. Neither vying for supremacy nor seeking validation through the approval of a spouse is healthy for a marriage. Only by surrendering our quest to find self-importance through human opinion can we establish an unshakable core identity based on who the King of kings and Lord of lords declares us to be.

Most of our family turmoil finds its roots in human pride and the hardened hearts that result. Unless we learn to move beyond pride, not only will a healthy marriage be elusive, we will also be blinded to the beauty of God's good design for humanity.

CHILDREN

The importance of the marriage covenant extends *far* beyond the relationship between a husband and wife. The human family, in its essence, was designed by God to be a covenantal entity. Family is that marvelous and mysterious enigma of humanity, by which two very different individuals bind themselves together and bring life into this world in the form of the cutest little self-centered sinners imaginable.

The mindset of the Biblical marriage covenant is intended to protect women who are physically and economically vulnerable, and who (literally) carry the weight of bringing children into this world. Furthermore, when the covenant virtues of faithfulness and lovingkindness wisely envelop a child, that little one is given the best chance of flourishing in this world.

Children are the most vulnerable among us, and family stability plays a critical role in early childhood development. This season of life sets the stage for the decades to come. Innumerable studies have shown the importance of the marriage covenant when it comes to the well-being of children in the home.[3] An article by Anna Sutherland on the Institute for Family Studies blog represents them well:

> Children are safest when they're living with their married biological parents—but if they're instead living with just one parent and that parent's partner (typically a mother and her boyfriend), they're more than six times as likely to be neglected and more than eleven times as likely to suffer abuse. Other living arrangements—with other married parents, unmarried parents, neither parent, or a single parent with no partner—fall somewhere between those two extremes. "Children do best with a mother and a father" may be a tired cliché, but it also appears to be true.[4]

Navigating the tumultuous waters of this world is difficult enough, and children who grow up in unstable homes enter those waters at a dangerous disadvantage. Of course, there will always be anecdotal outliers. Some children from single-parent homes, for example, will grow to be better-adjusted adults than some from two-parent homes. But as a whole, the trends do not lie. A traditional marriage covenant provides the best environment for a child to prosper in life. And if our children prosper, so does our culture. The reverse is also true; if our children grow up emotionally broken, all will feel the burden.

I know of a situation in which a mother—a drug user with a live-in boyfriend—had six children to three or four different men.

---

3. Information about congressionally mandated research concerning the incidence of child abuse and neglect in the United States can be found on the U.S. Department of Human Services website, https://www.childwelfare.gov/topics/systemwide/statistics/nis/.
4. Anna Sutherland, "Adrian Peterson's Son Not the Only Child Abused by Mother's Partner," Institute for Family Studies, October 14, 2013, accessed October 24, 2019, https://ifstudies.org/blog/adrian-petersons-son-not-the-only-child-abused-by-mothers-partner/.

The oldest lives with his father, having little or no contact with his mother because he attacked one of his younger sisters during a family "unification" visit at a therapist's office. The next oldest lives with his grandmother, whose lifestyle is no better than the mother's. He, too, has little contact with his siblings.

The next two are boys who are supposedly full brothers, but the younger one looks more like the boyfriend than his supposed father. Both of the little guys had lived with the mother and live-in boyfriend, where they were exposed to hardcore pornography before being old enough to attend school. The state got involved when the boyfriend slapped the younger child so hard that the red imprint of his hand was still visible when police arrived two hours later. That boy now lives with his supposed father.

The final two children belong to the mother and boyfriend and continue to live in their house, along with the other full brother. These three vulnerable and impressionable children have been in and out of the foster care system, often spending weekends with former foster parents who do what they can to bring some stability into their lives.

Do you find this brief summary confusing? Can you imagine the confusion, drama, and chaos into which these precious children were born? There have always been situations such as this, but when a society abandons a covenantal mindset and removes the Biblically-based moral underpinnings surrounding sexual relationships, these types of situations are much more likely to occur.

We can also add to our conversation the innate differences between a mother and a father in the parenting process. The male and female genders each bring a unique set of attributes into the family. The general combination of a mother's nurturing and a father's masculinity helps to make both boys and girls emotionally whole and secure. When either parent is lacking, children feel the loss. Certainly, a single Christian parent who prays for his or her children and diligently seeks God's wisdom for parenting will see Him work in ways beyond natural comprehension. Even so, the heavy burden that a single parent bears can be almost crushing at times.

We should render no judgment against those born into circumstances beyond their control, but it is vital to remember that broken children often grow to be broken adults, and broken adults hurt others, multiplying the dysfunction of a broken world. If there is one group that society should go to great lengths to protect, it is the children—the most innocent and vulnerable among us. When a large number of young children fail to experience the family stability necessary for healthy development, a nation flounders.

The importance of a stable family unit is well-understood among academic and political elites. A report by the U.S. Department of Labor released back in 1965 presented information about the growing crisis of fatherlessness in African American homes.[5] Not only is the problem now far worse, it has also spread to the populations of other subcultures.[6]

On just about every level, children benefit from having their mother and father in the home. But many of the people who could (and should) be improving the state of vulnerable children continue to disregard the centrality of the traditional marriage covenant to the well-being of children and the health of society. What are their reasons? Greed? Power? Self-actualization? We can only guess what drives the policy and decision-makers, but we can all feel the effects.

The social costs of a deteriorating marriage institution are staggering. Poverty, violence, and general criminal behavior all multiply when a culture lacks the mentality of covenantal marriage. We can bemoan the state of our world all we want, but little will change until we address the core issues.

The vast majority of mass shooters in the United States are male. A very high percentage of these young men grow up in unstable homes.

---

5. Daniel Geary, "The Moynihan Report: An Annotated Edition," *The Atlantic*, September 14, 2015, accessed October 24, 2019, https://www.theatlantic.com/politics/archive/2015/09/the-moynihan-report-an-annotated-edition/404632/.
6. Marjorie Valbrun, "Was the Moynihan Report Right? Sobering Findings After 1965 Study Is Revisited," *Washington Post*, June 13, 2013, accessed October 24, 2019, https://www.washingtonpost.com/local/was-the-moynihan-report-right-sobering-findings-after-1965-study-is-revisited/2013/06/13/80eac980-d432-11e2-b05f-3ea3f0e7bb5a_story.html?noredirect=on.

Included are school shooters whose fathers are absent, neglectful, or abusive.[7] Why do we spend multiplied millions of dollars on improved security while giving so little attention to strengthening families?

I have had the opportunity to view the issue of family from multiple vantage points. I grew up in an unstable home surrounded by many unstable homes in a housing project. In contrast, being blessed with a healthy marriage and the opportunity to raise two children of my own has helped me experience the joy of a healthy family life. Throughout the years, I have also spent a lot of time working with young people—many of whom would eventually become parents themselves. Through it all, the importance of God's wise and loving design is evident. *The healthiest environment for raising children is within the security and stability of a mother and father relationship—where two people are bound together in a covenant that is characterized by faithfulness and lovingkindness freely given.* Cultural trends will come and go, but our Creator's wisdom never wavers.

WRAP-UP

Regardless of our personal family experiences, the Lord's design is both compassionate and intelligent. At its core, family was meant to be a covenantal entity, a place where a high level of commitment provides the best opportunity for children to flourish and succeed. But a healthy marriage—and thus, a healthy family—requires more than commitment. Without the lovingkindness that characterizes God's covenants, everyone suffers.

The traditional marriage covenant might seem outdated in the eyes of some, but any culture that rejects God's gracious design for the human family is destined to cause harm to its children and tear itself apart at the seams. The marriage covenant is designed to provide security in the midst of human frailty in an uncertain world. The safest and most wholesome environment for children to be reared is

---

7. Emilie Kao, "The Crisis of Fatherless Shooters," The Heritage Foundation, May 14, 2018, accessed October 24, 2019, https://www.heritage.org/marriage-and-family/commentary/the-crisis-fatherless-shooters.

within a loving, stable family in which Mom and Dad each play their own unique roles.

I fully realize that our present reality falls far short of God's ideal. I understand the prevalence of blended families, and in no way am I suggesting that we treat them as second class. I recognize the painful reality of domestic abuse, and the need for a spouse to leave the home and seek help for safety's sake. I know the challenges of raising children, and that even the best parenting cannot guarantee the most favorable results. But I also know the Lord's desire to redeem, to take that which has been broken and to make it whole.

Yes, I readily acknowledge that, in our fallen state, life is far more complicated than it was in the garden of Eden. There is no such thing as the perfect family—even the best of us are flawed—but the family as an ideal is worth fighting for. God's good design has not changed, and I cannot help but wonder how much different our society would be if we all elevated the importance of the marriage covenant as a solid foundation upon which to build.

DISCUSSION

1. What makes the marriage covenant different from all the other covenants established by God?
2. Please read Genesis 2:18–25. What stands out to you?
3. Why are faithfulness and lovingkindness both integral to healthy family life?
4. Read Ephesians 5:22–32. How does the marriage covenant reflect the relationship between Jesus and His church?
5. What are the three aspects of a circumcised heart, and how does each contribute to the health of a relationship?
6. What are some practical things we can do to contribute to the well-being of children within our society?

Chapter Seven

OUTSIDE THE LINES

> *Or do you not know that the unrighteous will not inherit the kingdom of God? Do not be deceived: neither the sexually immoral, nor idolaters, nor adulterers, nor men who practice homosexuality, nor thieves, nor the greedy, nor drunkards, nor revilers, nor swindlers will inherit the kingdom of God. And such were some of you. But you were washed, you were sanctified, you were justified in the name of the Lord Jesus Christ and by the Spirit of our God.*
>
> 1 Corinthians 6:9–11 (ESV)

> The monstrosity of sexual intercourse outside marriage is that those who indulge in it are trying to isolate one kind of union (the sexual) from all the other kinds of union which were intended to go along with it and make up the total union.
>
> —C. S. Lewis

I love water! Not only is it my drink of choice, I relish being near bodies of water. Rivers, lakes, oceans—all are fine with me. My home area of western Pennsylvania gets its share of rainfall, meaning that we also have an abundance of streams and rivers flowing through the land. The result is a beautiful green countryside for a good part of the year. The seasons often bring spurts of heavy rain, and that can mean flash flooding. In an instant, homes are inundated and people sometimes drown. Peaceful, life-giving streams become torrents of brown death and destruction when they transgress their designated boundaries. So it is with sexual relationships.

From the beginning, the Lord established boundaries for the human race (Genesis 2:15–17). Grasping this truth is vital because we are not gods—the masters of our own existence. Instead, He alone is the all-powerful, self-sufficient, and sovereign God. He offers us abundant life, but true vitality depends upon us living within His designated boundaries. We transgress those boundaries at great peril.

THE MARRIAGE COVENANT AFFIRMED

My perspective is no aberration. Nor does it present an out-of-fashion ideal. We have already seen that the sovereign God alone possesses the authority to change the covenants that He has established. And any time God makes an adjustment, He announces the change. With the Lord's design for the marriage covenant, though, we find no change. None. Only reaffirmation.

- From the beginning, the Bible treated marriage as a covenant formed between one man and one woman.

- Except for the allowance of some divorce, the Mosaic law upheld the covenant.

- Religious-minded Jews, for the most part, upheld and honored the marriage covenant.

- Jesus reaffirmed marriage as a covenant between one man and one woman.

- New Testament writers upheld the marriage covenant.

- Early Gentile Christians broke ranks with their pagan pasts to embrace the marriage covenant.

From time to time, Old Testament Jews strayed from the one man–one woman marriage standard, but God never gave explicit approval for such actions. Furthermore, Jesus brought His followers back to Genesis' covenantal design so strongly that even His disciples struggled with the force of His language (see also 1 Corinthians 7):

> Some Pharisees came and tried to trap him with this question: "Should a man be allowed to divorce his wife for just any reason?"
>
> "Haven't you read the Scriptures?" Jesus replied. "They record that from the beginning 'God made them male and female.'" And he said, "'This explains why a man leaves his father and mother and is joined to his wife, and the two are united into one.' Since they are no longer two but one, let no one split apart what God has joined together."
>
> "Then why did Moses say in the law that a man could give his wife a written notice of divorce and send her away?" they asked.
>
> Jesus replied, "Moses permitted divorce only as a concession to your hard hearts, but it was not what God had originally intended. And I tell you this, whoever divorces his wife and marries someone else commits adultery—unless his wife has been unfaithful."
>
> Jesus' disciples then said to him, "If this is the case, it is better not to marry!" Matthew 19:3–10 (NLT)

These statements by the Son of God are heavy indeed. In essence, they affirm the marriage covenant, which was established by God in the garden of Eden as a lifelong union between a man and a woman. And because God is still God, truth is still truth. No amount of cultural change can alter His timeless design. Christ's response especially challenges our modern perspectives, but at the end of our era, we will answer to our Creator and not to the shapers of human culture.

When Jesus made His seemingly extreme comments about divorce, He was probably addressing a theological argument that had been brewing among Jewish religious leaders. One group felt that divorce was unacceptable, while the other made provision for a husband to divorce his wife for virtually any reason.[1] Thus, Jesus pronounced the practice of a man divorcing his wife to marry a more desirable woman to be an immoral violation of a sacred covenant.

Our Lord hates divorce (Malachi 2:16). This truth carries heightened meaning in cultures where women are particularly vulnerable. A male breadwinner who abandons his wife violates a sacred promise—one that he willingly made—before God. The Bible does establish some legitimate reasons for divorce, such as infidelity. Furthermore, the quest to be faithful to her marriage vows does not mean that a woman should accept abuse of herself or of children. Abuse is a gross violation of God's covenantal design and the sanctity of marriage, and a woman who leaves an abusive situation should find support—not condemnation—within the church.

God's ideal calls for one man and one woman to be united in marriage for life. Sadly, our experience is much more complicated in a world of shifting morals and ideals. Because of humanity's hardness of heart, it can be especially difficult to make a marriage work. As much as we hate the thought of divorce, both parties of the covenant must be willing to make extreme sacrifices, committing themselves to personal growth and humility. I do not say this as justification for the person who wants out of a marriage for selfish reasons, but to encourage those who find themselves in pain-filled circumstances they never thought possible.

Feelings of romance, of course, play a significant role, but the strength of a marriage is in covenant and not in romance. Sometimes, married life resounds with the harmony of a professional symphony. On many occasions, though, it resembles a preschool ensemble on steroids. It can take but a moment for the excitement of romantic visions to vaporize into stark reality.

---

1. Marvin Richardson Vincent, *Word Studies in the New Testament*, vol. 1 (New York: Charles Scribner's Sons, 1887), 108.

Our earthly relationships thrive only as they are characterized by the attributes of faithfulness and lovingkindness. While commitment is necessary for a relationship to endure, apart from lovingkindness, it rings hollow. We need both faithfulness *and* lovingkindness if our connections are to be emotionally healthy. Together they form the heart of a meaningful relationship—and especially those of the covenantal kind.

I once knew a Christian man who was incredulous that his wife would break the commitment of a sacred covenant by filing for divorce. But for years, that man had failed to treat his spouse with lovingkindness. She grew frustrated with the shallowness of the relationship, and he soon became single again. When faithfulness or lovingkindness is lacking from one or both partners, hearts once aflame with passion grow cold and hard.

The Mosaic law made provision for hearts growing cold, while Jesus called His people back to a true covenantal mindset with higher standards of faith and love. And because of Christ's teachings, the New Testament church treated the marriage covenant with the utmost regard. They recognized faithfully loving one's spouse to be a practical way of honoring their Lord. Early church leaders, who were representative of the people, were allowed only one wife (1 Timothy 3:2, 12; Titus 1:6). Also, the New Testament never describes marriage as anything but a sacred covenant union between a singular male and a singular female.

Where does that leave those who are either contemplating divorce or who have already traveled down that painful road? The marriage covenant is a sacred partnership between *two* people—each of whom possesses self-will. In other words, a spouse's thoughts and actions cannot be controlled. Neglect, abuse, bitterness, unfaithfulness—these are our human realities. And while I have seen struggling marriages marvelously restored through the prayers, love, and patience of a spouse, there have also been times when a marriage partner refused to consider the possibility of reconciliation. Such is the reality of our gift of free will.

Furthermore, as important as the marriage covenant might be, we dare never forget that the new covenant is the ultimate and predominant covenant. Those who have sinned can find cleansing and forgiveness through the cross of Christ. Does the modern church play too fast and loose with divorce? Yes! Should more couples take greater care to prepare for marriage through premarital counseling? Absolutely! But in the end, divorce is not an unpardonable sin, and forgiveness is available for those who have transgressed against God in the process. As Christians, our goal is to meet people where they are to help reconcile them to Christ—not to look down upon them with judgment.

THE SACREDNESS OF SEX

Think, for a minute, about what transpired in the garden of Eden. God created Adam as a lone individual. Then He made the one into two by creating Eve from Adam's side. Finally, the two were made one again through the covenant of marriage. Why would the Lord take such an approach? Why not simply make unisex humans who could reproduce by themselves?

There is something glorious about two free-willed individuals joining together to form a sacred, love-based bond. This points to sex as being a holy union to be celebrated within the boundaries of the marriage covenant. Furthermore, it is within such a bond that human life was designed to be replicated. Through sexual union life is imparted, and through covenant fidelity spouses are honored, and children are more likely to be emotionally healthy. Sex is sacred because it is tied to covenant oneness:

> Do you not know that your bodies are members of Christ? Shall I then take away the members of Christ and make them members of a prostitute? May it never be! Or do you not know that the one who joins himself to a prostitute is one body with her? For He says, "The two shall become one flesh." But the one who joins himself to the Lord is one

spirit with Him. Flee immorality. Every other sin that a man commits is outside the body, but the immoral man sins against his own body. Or do you not know that your body is a temple of the Holy Spirit who is in you, whom you have from God, and that you are not your own? For you have been bought with a price: therefore glorify God in your body.
1 Corinthians 6:15–20

Sexual immorality, in a New Testament context, is not a matter of law, but of covenant. Allow me to explain. The early Christian church became embroiled in a controversy when a group of "Judaizers" compelled Gentile Christian converts to be circumcised and follow the tenets of the Mosaic law as a requirement for righteousness. Paul and Barnabas were sent to consult with the apostles and other church leaders in Jerusalem on this important matter. The final resolution of their leadership summit had nothing to do with law and everything to do with God's covenants:

> "For it has seemed good to the Holy Spirit and to us to lay on you no greater burden than these requirements: that you abstain from what has been sacrificed to idols, and from blood, and from what has been strangled, and from sexual immorality. If you keep yourselves from these, you will do well. Farewell." Acts 15:28–29 (ESV)

The simplicity of this response is striking! The men who had walked with Jesus presented only a handful of essential requirements to the church at large. The use of blood possibly referred to mixing blood with wine for supposed vitality, and "what has been strangled" related to idolatry. Both are violations of a covenant relationship with God. Murder, if that is what the blood reference alludes to, touches on the Noahic covenant. Lastly, sexual immorality is a violation of the marriage covenant (see 1 Corinthians 6:9–11; 10:8, 11; Ephesians 5:5; Hebrews 13:4). The line between idolatry and sexual immorality is quite thin in the Scriptures. In fact, the Lord often equated idolatry with sexual immorality (see Hosea 1–3).

The term "sexual immorality" is translated from the Greek *porneia*, which originally referred to prostitution. I am compelled to agree, however, with the many Biblical scholars who proclaim that, in the context of the New Testament, *porneia* refers to virtually any type of sexual activity outside the boundaries of the marriage covenant.[2]

The early church leaders at the Jerusalem summit could have handed down a long list of rules; they had spent their lives immersed in the law-based culture of Judaism. Instead, they simply challenged God's people to remain faithful to His covenants. If believers young and old remained true to the covenants ordained by God, they would do well.

As a whole, the Western concept of morality has been turned inside out. During the past several decades, influential people have pushed the boundaries of sexual activity so much that what was once taboo has now become normal. A person needs only to compare a television show from the 1960s to a modern comedy to see how drastically the moral fabric of the United States has changed.

Concepts of human sexuality that had been integral to our society from its inception have now been redefined. Specifically, sex outside of marriage is no longer considered to be immoral if it is between consenting adults. What is considered to be cruel and immoral? Simply speaking for the exclusivity of sex within the traditional marriage bond of one man and one woman.

Is the Lord's design for marriage restrictive? Absolutely! That is the nature of covenant love. We willingly give up a part of ourselves for the promise of something greater. While some might see the command to avoid sex outside of marriage as a violation of personal freedom, it also means that a man who honors a covenantal marriage mindset will not violate women. He will not degrade or abuse his wife. He will not molest children. He will not contribute to the pornography industry by viewing their exploitive and degrading materials. He will

---

2. "What is the meaning of the Greek word porneia in the Bible?," Never Thirsty, accessed October 24, 2019, https://www.neverthirsty.org/bible-qa/qa-archives/question/what-is-meaning-of-greek-word-porneia-in-bible/.

not violate the sacred trust of his or another family by sleeping with a woman who is not his wife. He will not sexually harass women or use power in the workplace to arrange for sexual favors. And he will not traffic women for sex or provide a market in which they are oppressed.

We either proclaim ourselves to be gods and live according to personal desires, or with circumcised hearts, we worship Him as God and seek to align our lives with His good will. Self-centeredness, once embraced, opens the door for all kinds of unwanted consequences. Proverbs 5:22 tells us, "His own iniquities will capture the wicked, and he will be held with the cords of his sin." The context of this passage speaks about sexual sin, and in the end, a hedonistic heart will enslave both itself and others. *The greatest danger to human freedom lies not with the Christian religion, but with humans themselves.*

An erroneous understanding of God's grace tells us that we can engage in whatever conduct we desire and face no negative consequences. Truth, however, tells us that "Marriage is to be held in honor among all, and the marriage bed is to be undefiled; for fornicators and adulterers God will judge" (Hebrews 13:4). Will the Lord extend grace if we stumble? Absolutely! But the Holy Spirit within a Christian also provides the grace and strength to say "no" to ungodly desires. Sexual immorality—a violation of God's sacred covenantal design—is not an issue to be treated lightly.

We cannot go back and rewrite the past. In fact, accepting our unchangeable history is one of the most powerful things we can do. If we own the reality of our past, we can redefine the future by embracing God's good design for our lives. One of the most beautiful elements of the Christian faith is the ability to get a fresh start on a new path with a new mindset, and most importantly, in unison with the eternal Spirit of the living God.

HOMOSEXUALITY

Regardless of what cultural opinions might proclaim, the Bible consistently and uniformly presents homosexual activity as sinful.

This approach to marriage and sexual relationships has nothing to do with hate and everything to do with understanding God's design—and the loving wisdom that established it. As a Christian, my life is defined by what I am for and not by what I am against. The only reason I address the issue here is that it has become a terrible point of confusion—and contention—among Christians.

Just as no one ever starts out life with the intent of getting divorced or going bankrupt, neither do most people plan to have homosexual desires. The difference, however, is that while the Bible makes some allowances for divorce, it leaves no such room for homosexual practice.

With a desire to affirm those who seek to practice homosexuality and make room for them in the Christian faith, some religious leaders will call into question the original contexts and word meanings of several passages of Scripture relating to the subject. What they fail to address, however, is the *covenantal context* of the Bible as a whole. Both the Old and New Testaments were penned with the underlying mindset that marriage is a sacred covenant union, ordained by God, and entered into by one man and one woman.

The fact that Jesus never addressed homosexuality is more an argument *against* rather than for it. The writings of the Jewish Torah—Leviticus in particular—strictly forbid homosexuality (Leviticus 18:22; 20:13). Therefore, it was given no place in the Jewish culture of Christ's day. It does not matter if the concept of sexual orientation was absent in ancient times. If the Jews had somehow missed an understanding of God's design, or if He intended to change the definition of marriage away from the traditional view, we can be sure that Jesus would have spoken His mind on such an important covenantal issue. Instead, as we have already seen, when a group of Jewish leaders questioned Jesus about divorce, the Son of God confirmed the marriage covenant between a man and a woman so strongly that even His disciples struggled to process the ramifications.

I caution, however, that in considering the Biblical stance against sexual immorality, homosexual tendencies are not to be flippantly condemned. Sexual desires are some of the most powerful forces that affect humanity. Because of sexual lust, an exceedingly large number of people have traveled down long, pain-filled roads of regret. And while the male reader might never have burned with lust for another man, it is more than likely that he has battled against—and at times been overcome by—destructive sexual desires that lie outside the boundaries of the marriage covenant.

Our situation is further complicated by the fact that we live in a fallen world. A *creation-sin-redemption* pattern now defines our existence. God created everything to be "very good," but the Edenic crash polluted it all. Now, people are naturally born with a host of fears, quirks, and desires that run contrary to the Lord's design. Negative family and environmental factors can then further exacerbate our dysfunction. All the while, our good God seeks to redeem.

My heart breaks for people who are born intersex—with the formation of their sexual organs making their gender ambiguous. I also feel the pain of those who have struggled with homosexual desires or gender issues from a young age. In no way do I deny the reality of their experience. But this world has crashed, and just because we are born a certain way does not mean that God created us to be that way. Instead, the Lord seeks to redeem and restore all that has broken as a result of the Edenic crash.

I do not pretend to know the history, circumstances, and struggles of every person who reads this book and can speak only from personal experience. Upon birth, my heart was planted in a bed of weeds. From seemingly out of nowhere, feelings of fear, jealousy, and hatred began to grow in my mind. I did not invite those feelings, but I did allow them to take root in my thoughts. And when we allow a lie to take root, a tendency soon becomes our ever-present reality. Thankfully, I have found an amazing promise to be true:

> And we know that God causes all things to work together for good to those who love God, to those who are called according to His purpose. For those whom He foreknew, He

also predestined to become conformed to the image of His Son, so that He would be the firstborn among many brethren; and these whom He predestined, He also called; and these whom He called, He also justified; and these whom He justified, He also glorified. Romans 8:28–30

The key to fully realizing God's amazing promise lies in our response. Believing Romans 8:28–30 to be true, we can proclaim our love for the Lord by giving Him complete freedom to do what He wants with our lives. We can also set our faces to seek to know Him and His ways (Jeremiah 29:11–13). How many of us miss God's goodness because we refuse to seek and submit to His will?

No matter how much of a freak people declare you to be, and no matter how horrible you feel about yourself or your circumstances, the King of Glory has a meaningful plan for your life. And the more desperate the situation into which you were born, the more He will cause His glory to shine upon you. Even the best-intentioned person will disappoint, but our heavenly Father promises to bring you through—if only you will allow *Him* to write the end of your story.

THE SHAPING OF POPULAR OPINION

When I was a young Christian attending a state university, I joined a couple of friends in attending a meeting with a homosexual activist speaker. This event took place in the early 1980s (alas, I date myself), and the turnout was very light. Even so, the man remained undaunted. Brimming with enthusiasm, he mapped out a plan to make homosexuality acceptable to society. It involved infiltrating primary centers of influence such as the media, the courts, and the educational system in an effort to reshape public opinions about homosexuality.

Not too long after the visit by that activist, an article entitled, "The Overhauling of Straight America" was published. A book with further-developed content (*After the Ball—How America Will Conquer Its Fear and Hatred of Gays in the 1990s*) soon followed. Since that time, well-orchestrated media campaigns have focused on "desensitizing" the American public to the issue of homosexuality by using the six following techniques outlined in the article:

- TALK ABOUT GAYS AND GAYNESS AS LOUDLY AND OFTEN AS POSSIBLE.
- PORTRAY GAYS AS VICTIMS, NOT AS AGGRESSIVE CHALLENGERS.
- GIVE PROTECTORS A JUST CAUSE.
- MAKE GAYS LOOK GOOD.
- MAKE THE VICTIMIZERS LOOK BAD.
- SOLICIT FUNDS: THE BUCK STOPS HERE[3]

The intentional shaping of public opinion through the use of these techniques has resulted in many false perceptions about Christians who support a traditional Biblical view of marriage and sexuality. For one, we are often accused of focusing on the issue. But I know of many Christian leaders who address the issue of homosexuality only reluctantly. In doing so, the majority of these people are not creating a sole focus on homosexuality; they are simply responding to the focus that has already been created by the movement itself.

Other false impressions about conservative Christians are created through the use of *stereotypes*. In television crime shows, for example, the stereotypical homosexual is kind and generous—a good-hearted person who is in almost every way the victim of a cruel society. In contrast, the conservative Christian is typically portrayed as a hard-hearted, legalistic hypocrite.

Are there people who fit the stereotypical descriptions? Yes. But to say that all Christians are hard-hearted haters would be similar to saying that all homosexuals flaunt their sexuality while marching barely clothed in public parades. Instead, a large percentage of the supposed "haters" are deeply caring people who believe that the most

---

3. Marshall Kirk and Erastes Pill, "The Overhauling of Straight America," Gay Homeland Foundation, accessed October 24, 2019, http://library.gayhomeland.org/0018/EN/EN_Overhauling_Straight.htm.

loving course of action is to stand for God's good design even at the risk of being shamed and condemned in the court of public opinion.

I do not seek to stir controversy, but it is essential for us to know that the cultural shift away from the Biblical perspective of marriage and sexuality has been orchestrated by humanity and not God. If we study the progress of major cultural-political movements, we will find that many are tarnished by long trails of manipulation, intimidation, and bullying on the part of activists. Evidence of these dehumanizing techniques can certainly be found with the LGBTQ+ movement.

The cultural controversy of homosexuality also becomes a focus because this lifestyle is atypical compared to the majority. Anything outside the norm is given attention and judged. Some people are even inclined to overlook the significance of heterosexual fornication because they see it as normal, whereas homosexual activity falls outside of that sphere. From a Biblical perspective, however, *both* fall under the umbrella of sexual immorality.

People who have homosexual desires often feel condemned and excluded because they are labeled as "abnormal" or "broken," but we miss a huge point in all of this. *We are all desperately broken and abnormal in comparison to God's standard of righteousness* (Jeremiah 17:9 and Romans 3:9–18). There is not one human on the face of this earth who is not in desperate need of a Savior.

CAUGHT IN THE CHURN

When a ship travels across the ocean, it is common to see seagulls following. Why? With the force of propulsion, fish often get caught in the churn, providing an easy meal for hungry birds. Something similar happens with people who get caught between political movements; they find themselves being "chewed up and spit out." Today's political controversies over sexuality and gender are no different.

I have followed the arguments on both sides of the political fence. One side (i.e., what we call "liberal") argues that people are born with homosexual desires as part of their identity. But homosexuality is more of a behavior than an identity. And regardless of whether gay or straight, all who try to establish a flesh-based sense of identity will find themselves turned inside out and empty in the end. A truly secure identity can only flow from our relationship with our heavenly Father.

As portrayed by the imagery of water baptism, embracing Jesus Christ as Lord and Savior requires a "death" to our old way of living. This death is not physical, but rather involves a person surrendering his or her will to God. Accordingly, those who are unwilling to fully surrender their sexuality to the Lord will inevitably distort the teachings of the Bible on this issue. Their friends and family members face a similar temptation.

Do you remember the covenant between Israel and the Gibeonites? God expected that covenant to endure, and He brought judgment when Saul violated it. Nowhere do we find even an inkling of God altering the marriage covenant. What the Lord has established, no human has the right or authority to change. We must, with surrendered and objective hearts, allow the Bible to speak for itself, and what the Bible says is always in a covenantal context. Public opinion will shift with the winds, but God's truth remains eternal.

Those on the other side of the political fence (i.e., what we call "conservative") have been far too condescending for far too long. Truth without compassion does nothing to reconcile the world to Christ, and harsh rhetoric has driven many a struggling soul away from the good God that many conservatives profess to serve. Those who truly believe in the inspired authority of the Bible would benefit from embracing the sage advice found in Proverbs:

> Do not let kindness and truth leave you;
> Bind them around your neck,
> Write them on the tablet of your heart.
> Proverbs 3:3

Kindness and truth go hand in hand. Kindness without truth will lead people along a path of deception, while truth without kindness will drive them further from God's goodness. Neither blind compassion nor harsh rhetoric brings fulfillment of the Lord's loving purposes for human lives. We must have the courage to seek, embrace, and speak truth without malice or self-righteous indignation.

Certainly, these are difficult waters to navigate, but sexuality is an issue like no other. According to God's design, sexual intimacy is the culmination of other types of intimacy. In modern Western culture, however, physical intimacy is the starting point—and it often comes at the expense of experiential, emotional, intellectual, and spiritual intimacy. It is no wonder that, while sex can feel really good, people are so often left feeling empty and alone. Yes, sex is natural to our world, but we are of a higher order than animals. Sexual union was designed by our Creator with dynamics extending far beyond nature.

No matter what our human experience has brought us, we should all remember the words of Genesis 1:31 issued on the sixth day of creation: "God saw all that He had made, and behold, it was very good." In spite of the brokenness of our sin-riddled world, our Creator's design is still exceedingly good. If we want true life—a quest at the heart of sexual relationships—we will seek to align every aspect of our lives with His wise design.

WRAP-UP

When the Almighty finished His active work of creation on the sixth day, He declared all to be "very good." Dwelling in this sin-ridden world, and taking into account our errant desires, we can still live a highly blessed life by choosing to submit ourselves to His wise and loving design.

God's design for marriage calls for one man and one woman to be bound together for life in love and faithfulness. It is one thing to struggle with desires that transgress God's covenant boundaries and another to intentionally spurn the Lord's good design. For those who struggle, abundant grace is available. Those who spurn their Creator, on the other hand, are choosing to exchange eternal bliss for the momentary pleasures of this world.

Are you in need of forgiveness and cleansing? Meet Jesus at the foot of the cross. It does not matter where you have been, what you have done, or what has been done to you. You can drink deeply of His truth, and understand that you are *not* beyond hope! If you think that your sins are too big to be forgiven, or that you are a hopeless cause, you think too much of yourself and too little of the God who spoke our vast cosmos into existence with a few simple words. Our Creator's love, ability, and provision far exceed our shortcomings and needs.

Regardless of your past, your future can still be bright. The Lord still has a meaningful plan for your life, and the blood of Jesus—the sacrificial Lamb of God—has the power to cleanse all your sins and to wash you clean beyond human capability. We will learn more of this miraculously loving power in the pages to come.

DISCUSSION

1. Why is it necessary for all of us to have boundaries in our lives?
2. Please read Matthew 19:3–10. What is a hardened heart, and how does it affect a marriage relationship?
3. Please read Acts 15:22–29. How does the response from the church leaders relate to the covenants of the Bible?
4. What are some benefits of the restrictive nature of the marriage covenant?
5. How does a Biblical covenantal mindset affect our view of homosexuality?
6. In what ways can Christians do a better job of responding to those who live outside the lines of God's covenantal design?

PART IV
THE NEW COVENANT

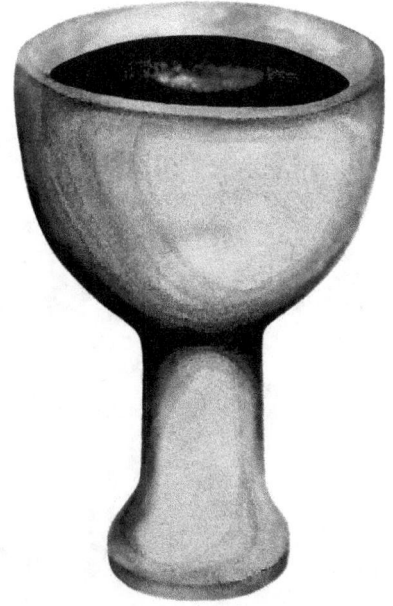

"This cup which is poured out for you is the new covenant in My blood." Luke 22:20b

Chapter Eight

THE NEW COVENANT IN BLOOD

> *And remember that the heavenly Father to whom you pray has no favorites. He will judge or reward you according to what you do. So you must live in reverent fear of him during your time here as "temporary residents." For you know that God paid a ransom to save you from the empty life you inherited from your ancestors. And it was not paid with mere gold or silver, which lose their value. It was the precious blood of Christ, the sinless, spotless Lamb of God.*
>
> 1 Peter 1:17–19 (NLT)

The most solemn truth in the gospel is that the only thing Christ left down here is His blood.

—D. L. Moody

One fateful night, desperate shrieks pierced the air of ancient Egypt. In every Egyptian household, the bodies of firstborn males, both young and old, lay motionless. Grief-stricken and terrified, their family members sobbed uncontrollably. No, the mighty nation had not been overrun by an invading army. Instead, a death angel sent by God had swooped low to bring judgment upon an arrogant, stubborn, and idolatrous kingdom (Exodus 12). There were no cries of grief, however, in the homes of Abraham's descendants. Hundreds of years of bondage under the hand of cruel taskmasters were finally coming to an end.

Jewish households were given the command to sacrifice an innocent and unblemished one-year-old lamb. The poor creature's blood was then spread around the door frame of each Hebrew house. The image created by the spreading of the blood resembled the shape of the Hebrew letter *chet*, which also means "life" to many Jews.[1] The sacrificial blood of an innocent lamb spread around the front door caused the wrath of God to pass over His people, settling instead on the heads of those outside of the covenant. The following morning, a ragtag group of slaves emerged victorious from the hand of an oppressive world power.

According to God's commandment, Israel commemorated this event by holding a yearly *Passover* celebration to remember the night that the wrath of God "passed over" their homes, and spared them. As important as the Passover was to Israel at that time, it also pointed toward an even greater eternal reality. That first Passover symbolically foreshadowed things to come—namely, Jesus Christ, whose spilled blood was to save another covenant people.

So far, we have reviewed the Edenic, Noahic, Abrahamic, Mosaic, Davidic, and marriage covenants. In addition to having a unique purpose, each covenant was designed to bring us to the greatest covenant of all: *the new covenant in Christ*. Before we address the most amazing compact ever formed, however, let us briefly review a little about covenants from our earlier chapters:

> From a Biblical perspective, *a covenant is a sacred and binding relationship of the highest order—a solemn pact or treaty*. A covenant is more than simply an agreement and also different from a contract. A contract is written in an effort to protect one's personal interests, often being subject to change or negotiation. Covenants, in contrast, are *unchangeable* and

---

1. "The Letter Chet," Hebrew for Christians, accessed October 24, 2019, https://www.hebrew4christians.com/Grammar/Unit_One/Aleph-Bet/Chet/chet.html.

established with a willingness to make extreme sacrifices for the sake of another person or group.

Covenants are marked by awesome blessings when they are honored and terrible curses when broken.

The establishment of a covenant usually involved a ceremony, which had the potential to create logistical problems when large groups of people were involved. For practical purposes, a *covenant representative* would act on behalf of each group. Those who did not participate in the actual ceremony were still bound by the terms of the covenant. The role of the covenant representative was vital, so that individual was required to have significant status and to be of the same blood as the group represented.

A blood covenant was considered to be especially sacred in ancient times.

While our modern view of ancient sacrificial practices often focuses on death, the ancient intent was to receive *life* in its full vitality. Through the life of the blood, intimate union with God (or the gods) and man was thought to be possible.

THE NEW COVENANT

The Lord created humanity in His image, intent on pouring out His blessings. Even with Lucifer's rebellion, the transgression of Eden, and the resulting curses, the Lord's plan to bless was not thwarted. Through the new covenant, those blessings are realized in a way that stretches the limits of our imagination. Let us consider Christ's words as He initiated the new covenant:

> And when He had taken some bread and given thanks, He broke it and gave it to them, saying, "This is My body which

is given for you; do this in remembrance of Me." And in the same way He took the cup after they had eaten, saying, "This cup which is poured out for you is the new covenant in My blood." Luke 22:19-20

One of the first things to understand about the new covenant is that it was *new*. The Greek word *kainos* would not be used to refer to simply a newer version of something old. It was used to indicate something completely new that had never been known before:

> As distinct from néos, "new in time," kainós means "new in nature" (with an implication of "better").[2]

The new covenant is new and unique—different from any other covenant. It is not a unilateral covenant, because though God carries the weight of the covenant obligations, we still play a role in participating. Neither is it a suzerain covenant because the Lord welcomes us as friends. At the same time, it is not a parity covenant either, because we can never be equal with God. Instead, the new covenant is comprised of various elements of the previous Biblical covenants, but with its own unique design.

Jesus is our representative in this new covenant, and when He established it, He used language that was reminiscent of past covenants (see Exodus 24:8). Christ's wording, combined with Old Testament prophecy (Jeremiah 31:31-34) and other New Testament events (Acts 10), announced that the new covenant fulfilled and superseded the old. So while its roots certainly stem from Judaism, Christianity is a religion unlike any other.

ONE WITH GOD

People often question the existence of evil in this world. After all, if God is both good and powerful, why does He allow evil to exist? In a

---

2. Gerhard Kittel, Gerhard Friedrich, and Geoffrey William Bromiley, *Theological Dictionary of the New Testament* (Grand Rapids, MI: W.B. Eerdmans, 1985), 388.

prior work, I explained three basic reasons that the Lord put the tree of the knowledge of good and evil in the garden: to establish much-needed boundaries, to provide the opportunity for humanity to love, and to allow for the temptation to be like God in a controlled setting.[3] A fourth reason is perhaps the most meaningful.

The Creator of all things wanted more than to simply *be with* humanity; He wanted to *be one* with humanity. The only feasible way to achieve such an intimate union is through what we call the "new covenant." Why did God not simply create us to be "one" with Him from the beginning? The type of oneness that the Lord desires must be free and motivated by love. A unity such as this reflects the relationship between the Father, Son, and Holy Spirit like no other can. This love is both pure and binding, yet still freely given.

The existence of evil on this planet is not a sign of an absent, impotent, or callous Creator. Rather, it reveals a love so powerful that it is willing to go through hell for the sake of becoming one with us. *Being one with us meant so much to God that He opened the door for pain immeasurable, even entering into that pain Himself.*

The heavenly Father wants us to understand deep within our hearts that the new covenant is a covenant of oneness. Mysteriously, humans can join with the Almighty God in an eternal spiritual union.

> Don't you realize that your bodies are actually parts of Christ? Should a man take his body, which is part of Christ, and join it to a prostitute? Never! And don't you realize that if a man joins himself to a prostitute, he becomes one body with her? For the Scriptures say, "The two are united into one." But the person who is joined to the Lord is one spirit with him.
> 1 Corinthians 6:15–17 (NLT)

Paul did not preach against sexual immorality to take away our fun and make our lives miserable. In these verses, he is guiding us toward a pure, unhindered relationship with our holy Creator.

---

3. Bob Santos, *Say Goodbye to Regret: Discovering the Secret to a Blessed Life* (Indiana, PA: SfMe Media, 2017), 74, 91–92.

How can we explain the opportunity for insignificant, self-willed humans to become one with the God who created hundreds of billions of galaxies with hundreds of billions of stars in each? How can we grasp a concept so profound that even angels stand in awe of our lofty status? Not easily.

When Adam and Eve ate of the forbidden fruit, their physical bodies did not die immediately. Instead, they experienced the essence of death—separation from God's presence. Thankfully, the Lord enacted a plan for reconciliation that went beyond merely restoring the God-man relationship. The Creator and His human children would now have the ability to be forever joined as *one*. The process begins by being born again—or born from above.

> Jesus answered and said to him, "Truly, truly, I say to you, unless one is born again he cannot see the kingdom of God."
> John 3:3

Upon being born from above, a person's spirit mysteriously *fuses* with God's. We still retain our humanity and never attain to the realm of divinity, but a mystical change takes place within:

> Therefore if anyone is in Christ, he is a new [*kainos*] creature; the old things passed away; behold, new [*kainos*] things have come. 2 Corinthians 5:17

The language of this passage again speaks of something new and different from what had been known in the past. Becoming a new creature in Christ is made possible only by joining in sacred union with the One who created us. This mysterious oneness between humanity and divinity cannot happen apart from the sacrificial actions of Jesus—God incarnate who established a oneness covenant of the highest order through His shed blood on the cross.

Upon becoming a Christian, you are still you. Your personality and natural affinities remain constant for the most part. For example, someone who likes to ride motorcycles does not suddenly begin to hate motorcycles. At the same time, the moral dynamics of life begin a radical transformation. And depending on how far into the depths of sinful living you were immersed, the newness of your life in Christ becomes more and more evident.

Throughout ancient history, cultures all over the world practiced blood rites with the desire to establish a "co-union" with their supposed deities. Recalling Trumbull:

> A covenant of blood, a covenant made by the inter-commingling of blood, has been recognized as the closest, the holiest, and the most indissoluble, compact conceivable. Such a covenant clearly involves an absolute surrender of one's separate self, and an irrevocable merging of one's individual nature into the dual . . . Man's highest and noblest outreachings of soul have, therefore, been for such a union with the divine nature, as is typified in this human covenant of blood.[4]

Many of the vile practices that occurred in ancient times were built upon an understanding of the importance of blood sacrifice. The essence of worship, however, was corrupted as people began to take the concept in directions never intended by God (e.g., human sacrifice or cannibalism). And like the pagans of old, modern men and women often seek to fulfill the innate desire for oneness outside of the boundaries of God's good design. Whether we speak of blood sacrifices or sexual immorality, charting a self-willed course for intimacy will pollute not only the fabric of our lives, but also the land in which we live.

The cultish activity of the ancients, bankrupt as it might have been, involved a quest to become one with our Creator. What even devoted religious effort failed to achieve, God provided as a gift through the new covenant. And the blood used to establish this sacred union was none other than that of Jesus—the Son of God. *The new covenant is the ultimate sacred bond—the covenant of all covenants.*

---

4. Trumbull, *The Blood Covenant*, 204.

THE LAMB OF GOD

Recognizing the new covenant to be a sacred blood covenant, we want to look more closely at the significance of the sacrificial death of Jesus Christ. When John the Baptist first saw Jesus coming to be water baptized, he proclaimed, "Behold, the Lamb of God who takes away the sin of the world!" (John 1:29). Inspired by the Holy Spirit, John recognized the connection between Jesus and the Jewish Passover lamb.

> Now the Lord said to Moses and Aaron in the land of Egypt, "This month shall be the beginning of months for you; it is to be the first month of the year to you. Speak to all the congregation of Israel, saying, 'On the tenth of this month they are each one to take a lamb for themselves, according to their fathers' households, a lamb for each household.'" Exodus 12:1–3

> "'Your lamb shall be an unblemished male a year old; you may take it from the sheep or from the goats.'" Exodus 12:5

> "'Moreover, they shall take some of the blood and put it on the two doorposts and on the lintel of the houses in which they eat it.'" Exodus 12:7

> "'For I will go through the land of Egypt on that night, and will strike down all the firstborn in the land of Egypt, both man and beast; and against all the gods of Egypt I will execute judgments—I am the Lord. The blood shall be a sign for you on the houses where you live; and when I see the blood I will pass over you, and no plague will befall you to destroy you when I strike the land of Egypt.'" Exodus 12:12–13

The Mosaic covenant was inaugurated with blood through a sacrificial system that included the Passover lamb. That first Passover marked the start of their yearly calendar, essentially transforming a people group into a nation. Those blood sacrifices atoned (i.e., made amends) for the sins of the people, thus enabling them to form a sacred bond with their holy Creator.

Again, the old covenant system of blood sacrifices was merely a temporary shadow intended to illustrate the power of a greater reality: *the forgiveness of our sins and the eradication of the Adamic curse are bound to the blood sacrifice of Jesus Christ as the eternal Passover Lamb of God.* When the blood of the Lamb is applied to our lives, the wrath of God passes over us, and we are spared the judgment that a treasonous covenant breaker deserves.

Over decades of ministry, I have heard many people say, "I don't spend time seeking God because I feel so unworthy of His love." And because they do not seek Him, neither do they serve Him. But even if they did, the service would be of a guilt-ridden, fleshly nature. What is lacking? An understanding of Jesus as the Passover Lamb.

When a Jewish man brought his Passover lamb to the priest, the priest *never* inspected the man. It was the sacrifice that God required to be innocent, perfect, and unblemished. All parties involved understood that the people who brought the animals were innately flawed. Indeed, their unworthiness was the very reason a sacrifice was needed. The blood of the lamb would cause the wrath of God to pass over God's covenant people, sparing their lives. It was the life of the blood that covered sin's death (Leviticus 17:11). And so it is that the life of Christ's blood cleanses our sins and makes us worthy to enter a sacred union with God. *If there is anything that will make us unworthy of His goodness, it is our stubborn pride that believes our sins to be more powerful than Jesus' blood.*

Our vitality finds itself in the spiritual substance of the eternal Son of God. Humanity has no spiritual life within itself, and without the sacrifice of Jesus, we would remain dead in our sins and eternally separated from the Lord. Such is our default state.

> So Jesus said to them, "Truly, truly, I say to you, unless you eat the flesh of the Son of Man and drink His blood, you have

no life in yourselves. He who eats My flesh and drinks My blood has eternal life, and I will raise him up on the last day. For My flesh is true food, and My blood is true drink. He who eats My flesh and drinks My blood abides in Me, and I in him. As the living Father sent Me, and I live because of the Father, so he who eats Me, he also will live because of Me. This is the bread which came down out of heaven; not as the fathers ate and died; he who eats this bread will live forever." John 6:53–58

Christ's words offended the sensibilities of Jews who understood something of pagan sacrifices. As a result, many quit following Him. But something greater was happening! The Son of God was laying down His life as an eternal sacrifice, so that through His blood humans could be cleansed from their sins to become one with God in a sacred union. Jesus was proclaiming a spiritual dynamic that most of those who were present failed to grasp:

"It is the Spirit who gives life; the flesh profits nothing; the words that I have spoken to you are spirit and are life." John 6:63

THE BLOOD OF JESUS

We have been given the gift of spiritual (eternal) life because of the shedding of the Lamb's blood. Let us consider some of the benefits we receive from that gift. The blood of Jesus:

- Cleanses all our sins.

- Erases our treasonous covenant-breaking history and causes the wrath of God to pass over us.

- Wipes away our guilt, cleanses our guilty conscience, and frees us from condemnation.

- Gives us confidence to draw near to God regardless of our failures, shortcomings, or imperfections.

- Makes us holy so that the Holy Spirit can dwell in our hearts. We become God's temples and new creatures, unlike anything this world has ever known.
- Brings us into covenant oneness with God.
- Elevates us to a position of high esteem by making us children in His royal family.
- Imparts to us the eternal life of the Almighty.
- Frees us from our debt to perfection.
- Enables us to abide in God's grace.
- Disarms the nature of sin so that it no longer has the power to dominate and control our lives.
- Brings us into covenant oneness with one another.

Any *one* of these items surpasses the value of anything we could find on earth. And here we have an entire—albeit limited—list of twelve. *Jesus established the new covenant with His blood, and that blood is our life.*

Some theological "progressives" have suggested that we do away with "all that gory and unpleasant blood sacrifice stuff," but that would be a mistake of epic proportions. Their line of thinking brings us back to the story of Cain and Abel:

> So it came about in the course of time that Cain brought an offering to the Lord of the fruit of the ground. Abel, on his part also brought of the firstlings of his flock and of their fat portions. And the Lord had regard for Abel and for his offering; but for Cain and for his offering He had no regard. So Cain became very angry and his countenance fell. Then the Lord said to Cain, "Why are you angry? And why has your countenance fallen? If you do well, will not your countenance be lifted up? And if you do not do well, sin is

crouching at the door; and its desire is for you, but you must master it." Cain told Abel his brother. And it came about when they were in the field, that Cain rose up against Abel his brother and killed him. Genesis 4:3–8

We cannot say with certainty why God rejected Cain's sacrifice. However, understanding the necessity of a blood sacrifice to atone for sins, we can build a strong case that Cain's sacrifice had a humanistic bent. Cain brought to God the product of his labors, but Abel brought sacrificial blood imbued with the life of an innocent victim. Devotion to God is never enough; we can only approach the Almighty on *His* terms.

Cain was the firstborn son of the human race, and in a sense, he represents all of Adam's descendants. When God said, "Sin is crouching at the door; and its desire is for you, but you must master it," He was speaking to all humanity. Sin is crouching at every person's door and desires to dominate us in every way, but we must learn to overcome. Mastery of sin, however, was not something that Cain could accomplish apart from a blood sacrifice—again pointing us toward the grace of God that comes to us through Christ's shed blood.

Even if Cain gave God his best, he did not give what was needed: lifeblood to cover the death of his sins. As a result, sin dominated his heart and compelled him to kill his brother. Abel's blood still speaks, however, telling us that we must meet God on *His* established terms of blood sacrifice—and of Christ's blood in particular.

We can also get involved with spiritual activity that is separate from our Creator, and thus devoid of truly substantive life. In this, Cain showed himself to be the first humanist. Those of his "spiritual lineage" are people with a high degree of devotion but who offer their sacrifices according to their own labors. As a result, their hearts remain uncircumcised, and deadly pride holds sway over their thoughts, attitudes, and actions. Worse still, those of Cain's lineage will judge and persecute those of Abel's lineage—the ones with humble faith who recognize their desperate need to be cleansed by Christ's blood and clothed in His righteousness. The attitude of the latter group echoes that of the apostle Paul:

> For since in the wisdom of God the world through its wisdom did not come to know God, God was well-pleased through the foolishness of the message preached to save those who believe. For indeed Jews ask for signs and Greeks search for wisdom; but we preach Christ crucified, to Jews a stumbling block and to Gentiles foolishness, but to those who are the called, both Jews and Greeks, Christ the power of God and the wisdom of God. 1 Corinthians 1:21–24

The cross is either a portal or a stumbling block. We either step into new life, or our self-righteous sensibilities take offense. *The issue is not whether we are good or bad people, but whether we are inside or outside of the new covenant.* The cross opens the door to God's covenant of peace, while rejecting salvation through faith in Jesus will condemn us to eternal unrest.

The fact that we have physical life confuses us. We live. We breathe. We laugh. We love. But our bodies also die. Even the greatest among us will grow old, wither, and pass from this world. The bravest. The boldest. The most beautiful. The most virile. The most intelligent and self-sufficient. Death is the great equalizer. From the least to the greatest, we will each draw a final breath, and then where will we be? Either inside or outside of the covenant.

Exactly how do we go from a state of death to "non-death" without an impartation of spiritual life? By default, we are dead to God, and by default, we will stay that way until we come to the foot of the cross. Without the blood of Jesus, we would all be eternally lost and dead in our sins. What person can declare to have lived sin-free? We have all stood in rebellious opposition to the King of Glory.

Christ's bloody sacrifice on a cross two thousand years ago accomplished what no degree of human effort ever could, facilitating a sacred union between God and humanity. While the Mosaic law allowed people to serve their Deliverer from a distance, the blood of Jesus enables us to enter into the most intimate union possible.

COMMUNION

The Lord commanded the ancient Jews to re-enact past events in an effort to recall their meaning and remember their significance. They recalled the past, but they also "brought the past forward" into their current lives so that its meaning would become a part of their mindset (see Leviticus 23:39–44 as an example). The Last Supper was a Passover meal, and when Christians celebrate communion, we are re-enacting the Passover meal that established the new covenant.

> When the hour had come, He reclined at the table, and the apostles with Him. And He said to them, "I have earnestly desired to eat this Passover with you before I suffer; for I say to you, I shall never again eat it until it is fulfilled in the kingdom of God." And when He had taken a cup and given thanks, He said, "Take this and share it among yourselves; for I say to you, I will not drink of the fruit of the vine from now on until the kingdom of God comes." And when He had taken some bread and given thanks, He broke it and gave it to them, saying, "This is My body which is given for you; do this in remembrance of Me." Luke 22:14–19

When Jesus said to His disciples, "This is My body which is given for you; do this in remembrance of Me," He might have had the tree of the knowledge of good and evil in mind. It would have been God's way of saying, "Let's start over and do this again. I am the Tree of Life, and if you eat of Me, you will find what your soul truly desires."

To give humanity a fresh start, Jesus took upon Himself the worst of our human experiences. The Son of Man was abused by Roman soldiers, tortured on the cross, and inundated with the weight of all the sins committed throughout our history. Jesus endured not only the depths of our suffering, but also of our shame—all with the purpose of "bringing many sons to glory" (Hebrews 2:9-10). What an incredible feat of love the Lord has accomplished on our behalf!

In celebrating communion, we are "drinking truth" by transporting the past work of Christ into our present reality. Doing so, we remember all that Jesus accomplished as our Passover Lamb. We also renew our faithfulness to the new covenant as an ongoing response to the extreme price that He paid on our behalf.

Communion is no mere ritual! To share in the body and blood of the eternal Son of God is a weighty matter. We dare not treat such a sacred bond half-heartedly, which is why the apostle Paul cautioned his Corinthian readers not to eat the bread or drink the cup of the Lord in an unworthy manner (1 Corinthians 11:27).

Part of partaking of communion in a "worthy" manner involves believing in and appropriating His work on the cross for our own lives. Again, if you think that your sins are too big for God to forgive, or if you think that you are too far morally gone, then you need a revelation—or at least a reminder—of the power of Christ's blood.

Celebrating communion reminds us that our right standing with God is based not on our own law-based attempts to find approval, but upon the all-powerful blood of Jesus. When we partake in communion, let us leave our guilt, shame, and condemnation at the foot of the cross, remembering the extreme sacrifice that Christ made for us. How foolish it is to wallow in guilt when He died for the very purpose of freeing us from condemnation. As we take communion, let us remember that Jesus allows us to start afresh, giving us the ability to step out of the shadow of the past into a bright, hope-filled future.

KOINONIA

Communion is no mere ritual. The Christian faith has always had our relationship with God as its central tenet. Celebrating communion should never be routine, but doing so on a routine basis reminds us that, through Christ, we have entered into a covenant of oneness with God *and* with one another:

> The cup of blessing which we bless, is it not the communion of the blood of Christ? The bread which we break, is it not the communion of the body of Christ? For we, though many, are one bread and one body; for we all partake of that one bread.
> 1 Corinthians 10:16-17 (NKJV)

The Greek word (*koinonia*) that we translate as "communion" speaks of intimate fellowship. Can we get any more intimate than being born from above in a covenant union with God?

> [K]oinōnía is a favorite term in 1 John for the living bond that unites Christians. It begins as fellowship with the Father and the Son (1:3, 6) by an abiding that commences here and is fulfilled hereafter (3:2, 24; 4:13). It issues in the family fellowship of believers (1:3, 7).[5]

Why do so many people run from relationship to relationship? Deep within their hearts, they long for an intimacy that only their Creator can provide. Sure, sex can bring pleasure for a moment, but a life of sexual abandon fails to fulfill. The reality is that sex will never be enough because no person will ever be enough. No human flesh can provide the spiritual oneness that can only be found through intimacy with our Creator. Ultimately, it is covenant oneness with God that we all desire—even when the true nature of our longings eludes us.

As always, faith is integral. Adam and Eve ate from the tree of the knowledge of good and evil because they did not believe that God—and all that He provided—was enough to meet their needs. They needed something more, or so they thought. Humanity has struggled with the same mentality ever since. But He is enough, and He knows our needs far better than we do. Celebrating communion reminds us of these things. Recalling the Lord's covenant promises and His faithful, loving character helps to transform intimacy with God from a wishful desire to a personal reality.

---

5. Kittel, Friedrich, and Bromiley, *Theological Dictionary of the New Testament*, 450.

THE NEW COVENANT IN BLOOD

WRAP-UP

The many ritual sacrifices practiced by humanity throughout the centuries provided only a faint shadow of the true substance of Christ's work on the cross. But regardless of how we feel about the concepts of blood sacrifices and covenants, none of us has the right to set the terms for our relationship with the Lord.

The new covenant is a blood covenant, but the blood shared is that of the holy Son of God—an almost incomprehensible reality. In short, there can be no higher covenant, no stronger bond, no more intimate relationship with God that is greater than the new covenant in Christ's blood. Perhaps this is why we are commanded to celebrate communion regularly. How easily we forget!

The Last Supper was a Passover meal, and Jesus died as the Passover Lamb. While the covenant-breaking world remains under the curse of God's wrath, those who have been cleansed by Christ's blood can dwell in peace. Through the blood of Jesus, and only through the blood of Jesus, we each have the potential to enter into a sacred union for which the deepest recesses of every human heart beats: a relationship of oneness with the God who created us.

DISCUSSION

1. Why would an all-loving and all-powerful God open the door for evil to exist in our world?
2. Please read Exodus 12:1–13. How does the first Passover in Egypt relate to the person of Jesus Christ?
3. What makes the new covenant different from all previous covenants?
4. List three benefits that we can receive from the blood of Jesus.
5. What is the purpose of celebrating communion?
6. Talk about something extreme you once did in the name of love.

Chapter Nine

OUR FOREVER MEDIATOR

For there is one God, and one mediator also between God and men, the man Christ Jesus, who gave Himself as a ransom for all, the testimony given at the proper time.

1 Timothy 2:5-6

Don't ever think that there are many ways to the Divine. Jesus is the one qualified mediator, the only qualified sacrifice, and the only qualified savior.

—Erwin Lutzer

Traveling through the interior of Africa in search of Dr. David Livingstone, Henry Stanley and his crew faced constant adversity. The terrain was treacherous. Wild beasts roamed the landscape. Food proved difficult to find. Bouts of sickness wore down their bodies. And tribal natives attacked their company. Finding the trek near impossible, Stanley began to make covenants with local tribes.

Covenant ceremonies were elaborate affairs, and it would have been impractical for potentially thousands of people to act at once. But there was no need. Each group chose a covenant representative to walk through the ceremony. That individual was a key leader in the tribe with authority to act on behalf of the entire clan.

On one occasion, Stanley made "strong friendship" with Chief Mata Bwyki who represented the Bangala tribe:

> "People of Iboko! You by the river side and you of inland. Men of the Bangala, listen to the words of Mata Bwyki. You see Tandelay [Stanley] before you. His other name is Bula Matari. He is the man with the many canoes, and has brought back strange smoke-boats. He has come to see Mata Bwyki. He has asked Mata Bwyki to be his friend. Mata Bwyki has taken him by the hand, and has become his blood-brother. Tandelay belongs to the Iboko now. He has become this day one of the Bangala. O, Iboko! Listen to the voice of Mata Bwyki . . . Bula Matari and Mata Bwyki are one to-day. We have joined hands. Hurt not Bula Matari's people; steal not from them; offend them not. Bring food and sell to him at a fair price, gently, kindly, and in peace; for he is my brother. Hear you, yet people of Iboko—you by the river side and you of the interior?"
>
> "We hear, Mata Bwyki!" shouted the multitude. And the ceremony was ended.[1]

Henry Stanley and Chief Mata Bwyki—the two men acted on behalf of their representative groups. Their blood was spilled and intermingled, but the terms of the covenant applied to the entirety of both groups. Understanding the role of a covenant representative shines a powerful light on the life and ministry of Jesus Christ.

God deeply desired to enter into an intimate union with His human creations, but two massive obstacles blocked the way. First, the blight of human sin clashes with our Creator's holiness. Second, if God established a covenant with the human race that depended upon our faithfulness, we would surely break the pact. A covenant with a perfect and holy God requires complete and perfect faithfulness. Who can meet such daunting standards? What person can claim to have never done a selfish deed, spoken a lie, or reveled in pride?

---

1. Trumbull, *The Blood Covenant*, 37.

OUR FOREVER MEDIATOR

Consider the covenants with God that we have addressed to this point. In each case, attempts at righteous living proved to be elusive; they also failed to extend beyond a few generations. Not one of those pacts was sufficient to be an end within itself. No matter how good we think we are, we can never meet divine standards of perfect devotion.

Furthermore, to violate a covenant with God is to bring curses upon our own heads. Consider what the Lord spoke to ancient Israel through the prophet Jeremiah:

> I will give the men who have transgressed My covenant, who have not fulfilled the words of the covenant which they made before Me, when they cut the calf in two and passed between its parts—the officials of Judah and the officials of Jerusalem, the court officers and the priests and all the people of the land who passed between the parts of the calf—I will give them into the hand of their enemies and into the hand of those who seek their life. And their dead bodies will be food for the birds of the sky and the beasts of the earth. Jeremiah 34:18–20

To sin against the King of Heaven is no minor issue, and only foolishly do we forget that vile curses are inflicted upon those who break sacred covenants—especially solemn pacts with God.

Do you remember the confident words spoken by the people of Israel both before and after the giving of the Mosaic law? "All that the Lord has spoken we will do!" But even before Moses finished carrying the stones of the Ten Commandments down from the mountain, the Israelites had already failed to obey by creating a golden calf to worship. For that transgression, they paid a steep price (Exodus 32). Three thousand men perished.

Are we much different from those ancient Israelites? An honest review of that simple Ten Commandments list will reveal our true spiritual condition. And indeed, this is the purpose for which the Mosaic law was given: to reveal our need and point us toward Jesus. *You and I are in desperate need of a Savior, and that Savior cannot be us.* No level of determined effort can fulfill heaven's requirements for perfect faithfulness and love, and no amount of self-sacrifice can atone for our sins.

OUR COVENANT REPRESENTATIVE

The Lord's keen eyes scanned the earth, through the corridors of time, to find a man or woman worthy to serve as a covenant representative for the human race. Our situation was hopeless; not one could be found. Not Abraham. Not Moses. Not David. Not Daniel. Undaunted, the perfect and holy Creator decided, "I'm going to have to go down there and do it Myself." And so He did.

Jesus became the answer to our dilemma. In Christ, we find both the cleansing power of divine blood and the perfect character required for a covenant with heaven. Becoming human, but never ceasing to be God, Jesus shed His blood as the unblemished Passover Lamb. And upholding the terms of the covenant without flaw, He became the "forever mediator" between God and humanity. Because of Jesus—the Son of Man—each of us now has the opportunity to relate intimately with the King of Glory.

God loves us all in equal measure, but it is not love that enables the guilty to stand justified in His presence. We owe that privilege to Jesus, whose blood was shed on a wooden cross two thousand years ago. The King of Glory is not only the God of love, but also of justice. If we understand the treasonous nature of our sinful pride—how it assails the very throne of heaven—we will tremble at the terrifying retribution demanded by true justice. Yes, it was love that sent Jesus to the cross, but apart from the torturous price that He paid, we would still be in our sins and separated from the life-spring of heaven.

Fathered by God but born to a woman, Jesus came to us as the "second" or "last" Adam. He lived in complete dominion over sin, succeeding where the first Adam failed (1 Corinthians 15:44–49). And because Jesus entered into our humanity, He could also stand as covenant representative on behalf of the entire human race. The

Son of Man then died as a *covenant breaker*. Taking upon Himself both the Adamic curse and our individual failures, Jesus shed His holy blood to cleanse our sins and obliterate sin's death by filling us with divine life. Thus, Jesus Christ—the Son of God and the Son of Man—established a sacred and binding blood covenant with God on behalf of the human race.

The new covenant was enacted between Jesus and the heavenly Father, while the Holy Spirit serves as the "Agent" who makes that covenant our personal reality. In many ways, we are like our father Abraham (and also Jesus' disciples), who fell asleep while the real work of covenant making was being done. Our role in the sacred relationship is simply to believe and respond.

Though it is no excuse for sinful behavior, we need not live perfect lives to be accepted by God. Our right standing with the Lord comes only through faith in Christ. Then, the patient and persistent Holy Spirit transforms us from the inside out.

JESUS OUR HIGH PRIEST

Not only is Jesus our covenant representative, He is also our eternal high priest—the forever mediator between God and man. Jesus has bridged the immeasurable gulf that stands between an unblemished God and sinful humanity.

Do you remember the story of Melchizedek and how he greeted Abraham after the defeat of the four kings (Genesis 14:17-20)? Melchizedek was a priest of "God Most High" and forerunner to the Jewish priesthood established through the old covenant.

The Jewish priests—all descendants of Moses' brother Aaron—performed a variety of religious and sacrificial duties so that God could dwell in the midst of the people without them being destroyed. Initially, it was a portable tent—later an elaborate temple—in which God's presence dwelt. The Israelites "lived in God's neighborhood," but only the priests were permitted through the door of His house. Thus, they served as mediators between God and humanity.

Within the Jewish temple, the Holy Place and the Holy of Holies stood as the most important rooms. The priests performed daily religious duties in the Holy Place, but the Holy of Holies was different. The presence of God dwelt there. Sacrificial blood and perfect preparations were required to enter His holy presence.

Only on the annual *Day of Atonement* (*Yom Kippur*) was one person—the Jewish high priest—permitted to enter into the Holy of Holies, which was separated from the rest of the temple by a thick curtain (veil) that acted almost as a wall. One day each year, the high priest drew near to God's presence to sprinkle sacrificial animal blood for the sins of the people (see Leviticus 16). Preparations had to be meticulous, for the priest risked the possibility of death if he failed to follow the ritual exactly. Ancient Jewish tradition tells us that a rope tied to the priest's body was used to remove his corpse if the bells hanging from the hem of his robe went silent.

Jesus was not a descendant of Aaron, but God proclaimed Him to be our forever priest according to Melchizedek's order:

> The Lord has sworn and will not change His mind,
> "You are a priest forever
> According to the order of Melchizedek."
> Psalm 110:4

High priests were limited by death from performing their duties perpetually. But Jesus, because of His eternal life and sinless perfection, was able to offer His own blood once and for all on our behalf. It is by His merits alone that we are given the extreme privilege of entering God's presence at will. The fact that the Lord would swear to Christ's role carries the weight of both force and permanence. Jesus is our high priest and the forever mediator between God and humanity. *Apart from Jesus, no man or woman, no matter how pious, can safely enter the presence of God Most High.*

> Therefore, since we have a great high priest who has passed through the heavens, Jesus the Son of God, let us hold fast

our confession. For we do not have a high priest who cannot sympathize with our weaknesses, but One who has been tempted in all things as we are, yet without sin. Therefore let us draw near with confidence to the throne of grace, so that we may receive mercy and find grace to help in time of need. Hebrews 4:14–16

Recognizing the role of Jesus as our high priest is essential to our spiritual health. Those who feel like spiritual paupers tend to run from God during times of personal failure, sinking low to wallow in their guilt and self-deprecation. That, however, is the worst possible course of action. *If our misery is self-inflicted because of our own sins, why would we think we can improve our situation by avoiding our Deliverer?*

I like to encourage people to take what I call "The Self Test." Very simply, we must ask ourselves if we have more confidence to enter God's presence when we are doing well than when we are struggling. For example, if I have had a tremendous week full of rich times in the Bible and sharing my faith with others, do I have more confidence to come before God than if I found myself frustrated, angry, and binge eating the ice cream I had just vowed to avoid?

If we feel more confident approaching God's throne when doing well, our trust is in ourselves and not in Christ. The truth is that we can come to God with the same measure of confidence *regardless* of how well we are doing because our right standing with God comes solely through our acceptance of Christ as Savior. Whether we feel great about our spiritual selves or terrible, we all have the same privilege of entering into God's presence through the portal of the cross. Always, always, always, no matter how well or how poorly we are doing, we approach God based on the merits of Jesus and not on our own.

Some people feel they need another intermediary in addition to Jesus, but you will find no support for this belief in the Bible. Imagine that you purchase an expensive item (such as a weed-eater) at a brick and mortar store only to find it defective. You immediately go back to the store, march through the doors, and demand to speak with a sales clerk. Meanwhile, the owner steps up and says, "Excuse me. I am the owner of the store. Do you have a problem?"

"I demand to speak to a sales clerk!" you reply.

"But I am the owner of the store, and I have the authority to correct any problem."

"Well, that's all well and good, but I don't feel important enough to speak with the owner. Please let me speak to a sales clerk."

"I really don't care how important you feel. As the owner, I am giving you permission to speak with me."

Does this exchange seem foolish? That is because it is. Praying to a saint or the Virgin Mary is no more rational. Our heavenly Father is the Owner of the universe and the King of this grand cosmos. His Son has paid a steep price to give you personal access to His throne. Why would you want to speak to one of God's "salespeople" when He is giving you permission to come directly to Him?

CHRIST'S HUMAN EXPERIENCE

As our eternal high priest, Jesus did something else that stretches the limits of our understanding: He gained *experiential* knowledge of our sin and weakness. Of course, God possesses the knowledge of all things, but He had never experienced all things. The Almighty had never been limited, or weak, or emotionally drained, or broken, or publicly shamed, or overcome by death. Jesus chose to experience all those things so that He might thoroughly understand us. *God does not just want to save us; He also wants to know each of us intimately.*

By crying out on the cross, "My God, My God, why have You forsaken Me?", Jesus was quoting Psalm 22:1 and communicating a crucial message to all humanity (see Matthew 27:45–46). "I understand! I get it! I know how it feels to be you. You are not alone in this. I am right here with you."

Why can Jesus, our high priest, sympathize with our weakness? He became one of us. Jesus Christ came to earth as *God incarnate* (in human flesh), and recognizing the nature of His humanity is vital to our spiritual health. Four specific facets of Christ's humanity stand out:

1. Jesus conformed Himself to the limitations of a human body. He came into this world as a baby to a relatively poor family that dwelt in an "armpit of civilization" town (see John 1:46). The Messiah lived in subjection to His earthly parents and other human authorities before beginning a Spirit-anointed ministry around the age of 30. Even then, Jesus could be in only one place at a time and was also subject to the need for food, drink, and rest.

2. Jesus was tempted in all things as we are and yet remained sinless. He did not encounter every exact temptation that we face. As far as we know, our Savior never had the opportunity to overindulge on chocolate mint truffles. Jesus did, however, face the types of temptation that are universal to all humanity.

   For example, the temptations of Jesus Christ in the wilderness (Matthew 4:1–11) were intricately tied to Adam and Eve's temptation in the garden. What would Jesus have been doing by surrendering to the devil's enticements? Joining the cosmic coup attempt! The Son of Man overcame where no other human could, and His actions turned hell on its ear. And while Adam and Eve were enticed under casual circumstances, Christ was tempted under extreme duress after having fasted for forty days and nights alone in the wilderness.

3. Jesus entered our shame. Immediately after eating of the forbidden fruit, the same Adam and Eve who had just been naked and unashamed now cowered in fear and shame (Genesis 3:6–7). In a frantic but vain effort, they tried to cover themselves using the fragile leaves of a fig tree. Since that time, humanity has struggled not only with guilt and condemnation, but also the pain and fear of shame that drive so many actions.

Why has our world seen so much violence—most of it perpetrated by men—throughout the years? Many factors are at play, but the fear of shame might trump them all. Public humiliation is one of the greatest fears to torment any man, and some will violently destroy another person's life to avoid looking bad themselves. How many men in our world would prefer to step onto a battlefield and risk death before entering the doors of a church at the risk of public humiliation?

From the time of His arrest until He drew His final breath on the cross, Jesus endured the depths of human shame. Crucifixion was not the result of Roman afterthought or divine shortsightedness. Indeed, the cross was designed to be an instrument of not merely torture and death, but also extreme public humiliation. The innocent King of Glory, who knew no shame and had no reason to ever be ashamed, allowed Himself to be abused and crucified naked, fully exposed as a vile criminal. Jesus knew exactly what He was doing; He endured the shame and humiliation of the cross so that He might understand us and also bring us into His glory.

4. On the cross, Jesus took upon Himself the full weight of our human sinfulness. The Son of God never sinned, but still, He knew sin and its effects intimately through His experience on the cross. The apostle Paul tells us that, "He made Him who knew no sin to be sin on our behalf, so that we might become the righteousness of God in Him" (2 Corinthians 5:21). What difficult words these are to fathom!

In becoming sin, Jesus experienced something that made heaven quake: He was, for the first and only time, separated from His relationship with the heavenly Father. It was something the universe had never known. And in crying out, "My God, My God, why have You forsaken Me?", the Son of God expressed the feeling of abandonment that all people experience as a result of the Edenic crash (see Matthew 27:46).

Because the Creator of our universe understands the weakness and frailty of humanity, there is no situation in which we cannot come to Him. No matter how much we fail, and no matter how deep we sink into turmoil, we can approach our high priest with complete confidence. *Not only has Jesus made a way through a sinless life and holy blood, He understands us and can deal gently with our struggles.*

IN CHRIST

While His sacrificial death was all that was needed for our salvation, Jesus chose to experientially enter into the fullness of our humanity. It was part of the *divine exchange* in which we also experience oneness with God by becoming "in Christ." As recorded in the Gospel of John, from the time that Jesus ate the Passover meal (as represented by communion) with His disciples, He emphasized covenant oneness:

> "Do you not believe that I am in the Father, and the Father is in Me? The words that I say to you I do not speak on My own initiative, but the Father abiding in Me does His works." John 14:10

> "I will ask the Father, and He will give you another Helper, that He may be with you forever; that is the Spirit of truth, whom the world cannot receive, because it does not see Him or know Him, but you know Him because He abides with you and will be in you. I will not leave you as orphans; I will come to you." John 14:16–18

> "In that day you will know that I am in My Father, and you in Me, and I in you." John 14:20

What is significant about the heart that beats within your chest? It is *your* heart because it is *in you*. Similarly, when we think about being in Christ, the Lord treats us as a part of His own body. All the lovingkindness that the heavenly Father would extend to Jesus, He now extends to us. Just as we were "in" Adam, we are now "in" Christ.

The idea of God and humans becoming unified in spirit has been the desire of both parties since age eternal. The human race has tried all manner of rituals and blood sacrifices to become one with its Creator, while God set into motion a profound plan to send Jesus as our perfect covenant representative.

Having entered into covenant oneness with God, all Christians are now in Christ, and it is because we are in Him that we are clothed in spiritual robes of righteous perfection, made worthy to receive the many blessings of this covenant union. The famed preacher Charles Spurgeon once said, "You stand before God as if you were Christ, because Christ stood before God as if he were you—he in your stead, you in his stead."[2]

Religiously minded people often try to earn God's acceptance. But as Christians, we are *already* in Christ because we were baptized into the new covenant. In his letter to the Ephesian church, the apostle Paul tells us:

> For by grace you have been saved through faith; and that not of yourselves, it is the gift of God; not as a result of works, so that no one may boast. Ephesians 2:8–9

No number of good deeds can gain us God's approval, but through His grace, we find a powerful platform for acceptance. This means that the pressure is off! *Our Creator simply calls us to live out of the lofty position that we already have, rather than trying to attain some special status in His eyes* (see Ephesians 2:1–6).

As the children of God, it is vital that we develop an "in-Christ" mindset. When we consider our lives, there is no part of our existence that is removed from God's nearness. The need for provision. Stepping out of our comfort zones. Working through difficult situations. Every element of our lives is wrapped up with us being in Christ and Christ being in us. The Bible tells us:

---

2. C. H. Spurgeon, "Justification by Faith" (sermon, Metropolitan Tabernacle, London, April 28, 1867), accessed October 24, 2019, http://www.romans45.org/spurgeon/sermons/3392.htm.

Therefore there is now no condemnation for those who are in Christ Jesus. For the law of the Spirit of life in Christ Jesus has set you free from the law of sin and of death. Romans 8:1–2

In Him we have redemption through His blood, the forgiveness of our trespasses, according to the riches of His grace which He lavished on us. Ephesians 1:7–8a

In Him, you also, after listening to the message of truth, the gospel of your salvation—having also believed, you were sealed in Him with the Holy Spirit of promise, who is given as a pledge of our inheritance, with a view to the redemption of God's own possession, to the praise of His glory. Ephesians 1:13–14

For He rescued us from the domain of darkness, and transferred us to the kingdom of His beloved Son, in whom we have redemption, the forgiveness of sins. Colossians 1:13–14

Of this church I was made a minister according to the stewardship from God bestowed on me for your benefit, so that I might fully carry out the preaching of the word of God, that is, the mystery which has been hidden from the past ages and generations, but has now been manifested to His saints, to whom God willed to make known what is the riches of the glory of this mystery among the Gentiles, which is Christ in you, the hope of glory. Colossians 1:25–27

Becoming a Christian involves more than being forgiven of our sins so that we can go to heaven—as great as that is. *The ultimate purpose of life is an intimate union with the God who created us.*

Sadly, even though we are made one with God through the new covenant in Christ, we do not always live in His presence. One of the secrets to experiencing the Lord's vitality involves a process of *aligning* and *abiding*. The burden of perfection falls upon Jesus, but He also reminds us that we play a role in abiding in His presence:

> "I am the vine, you are the branches; he who abides in Me, and I in him, bears much fruit; for without Me you can do nothing." John 15:5

> "As the Father loved Me, I also have loved you; abide in My love. If you keep My commandments, you will abide in My love, just as I have kept My Father's commandments and abide in His love." John 15:9-10

I have been married long enough to know that two people can live together without truly relating to one another. If we are not careful, Debi and I can find ourselves always busy and distracted, focused on one thing or another, but not really communicating. This is especially true if a husband and wife differ in their thought patterns—a typical problem between the sexes. And if a couple allows their emotional disconnect to linger, their relationship will decay to where they cease to "abide" with one another even while living in the same house.

Similarly, a person can be a Christian and not abide in an active relationship with the Lord. Because of our natural thought patterns, *by default*, we are out of alignment with God's design. For example, the Scriptures teach that our spiritual existence is of a higher order than the natural. But when we naturally place our primary focus on physical elements of life such as appearance, wealth, and success, we fall out of sync with His wise design. Only as we begin to change our thinking—and our actions follow in obedience to God—will we find ourselves abiding (dwelling) in His presence. It is out of this abiding relationship that spiritual fruit is then borne.

The secret to a blessed life is to abide in Christ, and to abide we must obey the Lord's command to believe (John 6:29; 14:1). But God does not just call us to believe in a nebulous sense; our quest is to trust Him with our entire hearts through all the adversities that are so common to our world. That is why reading the Bible is necessary for good spiritual health. His Word proclaims what to believe. Life transformation is then activated as we discover what it means to be in Christ, fully embracing those things that are true.

WRAP-UP

So much more could be said about Jesus as our high priest and about being in Christ, but for now, let us keep the following in mind:

- The entire Bible was written in a covenantal context.

- Jesus is the unblemished Lamb of God whose blood has the power to cleanse every sin.

- Jesus is the perfect covenant representative for humanity who upholds all the requirements of the covenant without fail.

- Jesus is the perfect high priest because He lowered Himself to take human form, and because of the power of an indestructible life that could not be quenched.

- Jesus experientially understands our weaknesses, temptations, and sins.

- The Christian life involves more than being forgiven of our sins and going to heaven. The Lord wants us to know Him intimately. This is the essence of eternal life.

- Though we are made one with God through the new covenant, an abiding relationship—and therefore a fruitful life—requires that we respond with faith to these and other Biblical truths.

DISCUSSION

1. How do the Ten Commandments reveal our need for God?
2. Talk about the role and purpose of a covenant representative. Why is it foolish to look to any mediator other than Jesus?
3. What is the effect of knowing that Jesus understands our every struggle?
4. Talk about your own life and how you would do with the "Self Test" relating to Hebrews 4:14–16.

5. What is the significance of being in Christ?
6. What are some keys to abiding in Christ?

Chapter Ten

BOUND BY LOVE

For you were called to freedom, brethren; only do not turn your freedom into an opportunity for the flesh, but through love serve one another. For the whole Law is fulfilled in one word, in the statement, "You shall love your neighbor as yourself."

Galatians 5:13–14

Love is the only fire that is hot enough to melt the iron obstinacy of a creature's will.

—Alexander MacLaren

Immediately after graduating from college, James "Maggie" Megellas accepted a commission as a second lieutenant in the U.S. Army during World War II.[1] Volunteering to be a paratrooper, Maggie became the most decorated officer in the history of the Army's 82nd Airborne Division.

Though wounded twice, he fought for days on end against hardened Nazi forces in Italy. Megellas then parachuted into Holland

---

1. David Tarrant, "Why a 101-Year-Old World War II Hero Says His Is Not the 'Greatest Generation,'" *Dallas Morning News*, May 23, 2018, accessed October 25, 2019, https://www.dallasnews.com/news/us-news/2018/05/23/world-war-ii-hero-now-101-says-peace-new-mission.

as part of Operation Market Garden—an ill-famed mission to secure a group of bridges. The young leader and his men joined others in paddling 1,200 feet across a swift river in flimsy canvas boats—all in broad daylight and under intense machine-gun fire. This feat was followed by crossing several hundred yards of barren landscape to storm a castle held by the Nazis. Just a few days later, Maggie again risked his life to attack an enemy force, rescuing three prisoners in the process. Withdrawing through enemy lines, the fearless leader carried a wounded man, firing his submachine gun with one hand.

One of the most deadly battles of the war came not long after. Having routed a large Nazi force in the Ardennes Forest during the Battle of the Bulge, Megellas and his men found themselves under attack by a German Panther tank. While everyone else scattered in fear, Maggie disabled the tank's track with a grenade and then put it out of commission by dropping another one down the turret.

As the war ground toward an end, Megellas and his men found themselves helping to liberate a concentration camp in northern Germany. According to Maggie himself, "That's when we realized the greater cause we were fighting for. We were fighting for the values that we believed in as Americans."

When soldiers fight for the flag of the United States of America, they fight for all the flag represents, and specifically, for the U.S. Constitution. Though not all the framers of this unique document could be considered Christian, their work was deeply influenced by the Bible. The First Amendment to the Constitution reads:

> Congress shall make no law respecting an establishment of religion, or prohibiting the free exercise thereof; or abridging the freedom of speech, or of the press; or the right of the people peaceably to assemble, and to petition the Government for a redress of grievances.[2]

The *very first* article of the *First* Amendment establishes *the freedom of religion*. This was no accident or oversight. Men who had seen

---

2. U.S. Constitution, Amendment I

and experienced decades of tyranny recognized the free exercise of religion to be one of the cornerstones of freedom itself. And the religion they had in mind was Christianity because it is within the Christian faith that we discover the true essence of freedom.

OUT OF EDEN

For many people, the garden of Eden remains a mystery. Created in glory and planted in paradise, humanity could not have been given a better start. *But*—and that is a much larger word than its three-letter length—God mysteriously placed both the tree of life and the tree of the knowledge of good and evil within easy access. The lone restriction was to refrain from eating the fruit of the latter tree.

Humans were created in the image of God, and the Bible tells us that "God is love" (1 John 4:8). By its very nature, love must be free. Of course, giving someone the freedom to love means also giving that person the freedom not to love. It is the ability to choose that infuses love with majestic beauty—but also profound pain.

We dare not overlook the fact that Adam and Eve ate from "the tree of the knowledge of good and evil" and not "the tree of the knowledge of evil." This means that *the knowledge of good can be just as deadly as the knowledge of evil.* Such a seemingly bizarre thought makes more sense when we take human pride into account. When the perception of self-good leads us to exalt ourselves, we launch an assault against the throne of heaven!

The Lord put before the human race a choice between life and death. In choosing the "death tree," they sought to go rogue, seeking independence from God, while joining a treasonous assault against His throne. Central to this effort was a desire to find goodness and glory within themselves, apart from their Creator. At this moment, their eyes became aware of, and their souls bound to, God's standards of perfection. These, of course, were standards they could never meet.

The progression of this story brings us to yet another human mystery: the conscience. Unlike any other creature on earth, humans possess an internal moral law. But unlike the other laws of our cosmos, the conscience is powerless to create action. Our internal compass might tell us what is "good" and what is "bad," but it will not force us to act in either way. Also, the conscience is malleable; its standards can be "programmed." For example, due to cultural influences, sex outside of marriage stirs guilt in some people but elicits not even a twinge of remorse of others.

In addition to seeking to be like God apart from God, Adam and Eve saw that "the tree was good for food, and that it was a delight to the eyes, and that the tree was desirable to make one wise" (Genesis 3:6). In other words, the tree held a powerful appeal. In this, God understood something that humanity still struggles to grasp: the allure of the tree of the knowledge of good and evil would forever appeal to human desire until we fully experienced its bitter effect.

Here we find a puzzle that has befuddled humanity since the day that our ancestors ate of the forbidden fruit. Moral laws are needed to maintain social order, but neither they nor religious rituals can bring us nearer to God. Neither can they elevate us in His sight. If we want to abide in the Lord's presence, our hearts must be circumcised so that we are no longer driven by the self-centered, self-willed, and self-glorifying motivations that flow from seeking to be like God apart from God. Lasting glory comes not from our ability to measure up to standards, but from the indwelling presence of the Holy Spirit.

INTO A MINISTRY OF DEATH

The old and new covenants serve as expressions of the two trees that stood in Eden. The Mosaic law represents the tree of the knowledge of good and evil with all its standards, while Jesus is our "tree" of everlasting life.

Since the moment Adam and Eve ate from the tree of the knowledge of good and evil, humanity has been driven by a compulsion to meet standards. In essence, this is the prideful quest to achieve status by being better than others. If we perceive that we meet the standards of God and humanity—whatever they might be—we are good, we are acceptable, we are significant. In contrast, if we fail, we feel guilty, condemned, and ashamed. Regardless of our perceived success or failure, however, those who seek to be righteous by law-based self-effort will find themselves *bound* by the power of sin.

Our existence in this world becomes stressful, disheartening, burdensome, and exhausting when we feel that we cannot live up to a vast array of human and divine expectations. Our cultural mores make us feel as though we are never enough—that we are never good enough, never giving enough, and never doing enough. Furthermore, the Ten Commandments were engraved on *stone* tablets, signifying that law-based demands are unyielding. They send an unbending message: "Rise and meet the standards or face severe consequences!"

The timing of the Mosaic law was not arbitrary. It came on the heels of the exodus from Egypt, where God's people had lived as oppressed slaves. The cruel whip of taskmasters demanded that quotas be met, but without the means to do so. The following verse, which is probably the combined work of multiple sources, speaks volumes:

> Run, John, run, the law commands
> But gives us neither feet nor hands,
> Far better news the gospel brings:
> It bids us fly and gives us wings.
> A rigid matter was the law, demanding brick, denying straw,
> But when with gospel tongue it sings, it bids me fly and gives me wings.[3]

The law demands that we meet its requirements, but it provides no ability to do so. Thus, apart from Christ, we owe an unpayable debt to perfection, and the dogmatic standards of law condemn us when we fail to deliver. Furthermore, we need to break only one law to be declared a "lawbreaker." That which is intended to be a good guide to

---

3. Justin Taylor, "Run John Run," TGC The Gospel Coalition, July 27, 2011, accessed October 25, 2019, https://www.thegospelcoalition.org/blogs/justin-taylor/run-john-run/.

our behavior ultimately works against us because we lack the power to obey its requirements.

We must remember, however, that the primary problem lies not with law itself, but with the nature of sin. Through an awareness of good and evil, our sin-nature causes us to strive for godhood, compelling us to meet standards of perfection. Seeking to be the highest authority, our fallen nature also rebels against being told what to do. I once saw a photo of a long drainage pipe extending into the ocean, guarded by a sign that read, "Do not play on pipe." Not surprisingly, children were draped all over the pipe, while the rest of the ocean remained child-free. As much as we want to celebrate human goodness, our race is at war with its Creator.

What God began in the paradise of Eden, He plans to complete in the paradise of heaven. But if He were to allow humans into heaven with unchanged hearts, that eternal utopia would risk the same corruption that has devastated our planet. This reveals another primary purpose of the Mosaic covenant: to so satiate us with the slavery, judgment, guilt, condemnation, and frustration that come from seeking righteousness by law that we would tenaciously lay hold of the new covenant in Christ and never let go.

> For if a law had been given which was able to impart life, then righteousness would indeed have been based on law. But the Scripture has shut up everyone under sin, so that the promise by faith in Jesus Christ might be given to those who believe.
>
> But before faith came, we were kept in custody under the law, being shut up to the faith which was later to be revealed. Therefore the Law has become our tutor to lead us to Christ, so that we may be justified by faith. Galatians 3:21b–24

The old covenant proved imperfect because it depended upon an "outside-in" process to relate to God. Opposite its apparent intent, the Mosaic law helped to fuel sinful desires. Why? The quest to find righteousness by meeting standards has its roots in the tree of the knowledge of good and evil. The attempt, by self-effort, to meet law-based standards of righteous perfection leads to captivity and death for even spiritually minded people. As the apostle Paul wrote:

> You are our letter, written in our hearts, known and read by all men; being manifested that you are a letter of Christ, cared for by us, written not with ink but with the Spirit of the living God, not on tablets of stone but on tablets of human hearts.
>
> Such confidence we have through Christ toward God. Not that we are adequate in ourselves to consider anything as coming from ourselves, but our adequacy is from God, who also made us adequate as servants of a new covenant, not of the letter but of the Spirit; for the letter kills, but the Spirit gives life. 2 Corinthians 3:2–6

Paul goes on to describe the Mosaic law as a ministry of "death" and "condemnation." Does that not call to mind the tree of the knowledge of good and evil? *In giving the Mosaic law and its many standards, the Lord was relating to the human race according to the mindset that we chose in the garden of Eden.* And just like the tree of the knowledge of good and evil, the Mosaic law promises life but instead delivers death. Making us aware of our sins and shortcomings, living by law for the sake of righteousness adds fuel to the flames of sin.

CULTURAL LEGALISM

The human conscience and the Mosaic law both trace their roots to the tree of the knowledge of good and evil, but a third element of law also warrants mention: *cultural legalism*. We can define legalism as "strict, literal, or excessive conformity to the law or to a religious or moral code."[4] Cultural legalism invokes the unwritten standards (laws) of our contemporary culture. It is a world in which people must conform to cultural standards if they are to be accepted and approved.

---

4. Merriam-Webster, s.v. "legalism," accessed October 25, 2019, https://www.merriam-webster.com/dictionary/legalism.

For decades, families in the United States enjoyed the annual tradition of watching the Christmas special, *Rudolph the Red-Nosed Reindeer*. This animated tale, which was produced in a different era, tells the story of a reindeer reject who overcomes all manner of adversity to emerge an unlikely hero. One year, however, cultural legalists decided that *Rudolph the Red-Nosed Reindeer* did not meet their self-imposed standards. Suddenly, we were told to avoid the children's show because it is homophobic, misogynistic, and supports bullying. In essence, these new cultural guidelines of political correctness were no different from those of the religious legalists— except that they lacked the use of a religious text to define the acceptable standards. Instead, the rules were merely social constructs forced upon the general population.

These types of situations have flooded our modern era, and we are constantly adjusting what is and is not "acceptable" behavior according to current cultural norms. Without a solid stronghold on which to base our truth (the Bible), our cultural moral constructs will ever change with the tides of human opinion.

Political correctness is a form of cultural legalism, driven by fear and condemnation. Expectations are high and the backlash harsh for those who fail to meet the requirements of this ever-changing code. And though we proclaim to have the freedom to do as we will, our cultural slave masters compel us to walk a very specific, narrow, and anxious line. There is no grace for those outside the sphere of cultural conformity. Whether with chains or with fear, living under law and without grace strips the freedoms so graciously given to us by God.

When immersed in cultural legalism, we see wrong virtually everywhere we look. This person has this fault and that person another. Before we know it, we find ourselves isolated and alone because no person (or church) can meet our standards. Eventually, our world can become so small that we ourselves have no room to move.

Cultural legalism is also common in religious environments, including evangelical ones where grace is preached. Our bond of Christian unity *should* be cemented with love (Colossians 3:14). With legalism, however, peace and unity are dependent upon *uniformity*. People are excluded because they do not pray, worship, or dress the "right" way. They do not use the right Bible or conform to the right teaching style. They do not parent the right way. And of course, their theology is suspect because they are not part of a denomination that sees things the right way. Like the Pharisees of old, religious legalists bind people as slaves. Ironically, religious legalists are of the same spirit as the mainstream cultural legalists who so often oppose them.

GOD'S AMAZING SOLUTION

Our human way of thinking causes us to live from an outside-in approach. Standards of all kinds are thrust upon us, and we are required—or should we say enslaved?—to measure up to those standards in order to be accepted (i.e., righteous). Is this not how the Mosaic law functioned? God's design for the new covenant, however, works from the inside out:

> "Behold, days are coming," declares the Lord, "when I will make a new covenant with the house of Israel and with the house of Judah, not like the covenant which I made with their fathers in the day I took them by the hand to bring them out of the land of Egypt, My covenant which they broke, although I was a husband to them," declares the Lord. "But this is the covenant which I will make with the house of Israel after those days," declares the Lord, "I will put My law within them and on their heart I will write it; and I will be their God, and they shall be My people." Jeremiah 31:31–33

The Almighty's solution to our law-based thinking is the gospel of Jesus Christ, which serves as the perfect antidote for human pride. Humanity is enslaved by the need to measure up to law-based standards of perfection, and the Mosaic law declares all of us guilty. Even every "good" person standing in opposition to God would appear as a pile of rotting flesh opposite a glorious, majestic lion. Thankfully, we also have the promise that, through faith in Jesus, we can be glorious as well. Glory beside glory—or better yet—our glory as a reflection of His.

Under the new covenant, the burden of perfection falls upon Jesus and not upon us. He is the perfect sacrifice, without flaw or blemish. When we are cleansed by His blood and abide in His grace, we can begin to live life from the inside out, with a grace-imbued vigor that flows from the throne of heaven.

The grace of Christ frees us from the sinful tendencies rooted in the tree of the knowledge of good and evil, returning us to the tree of life. All people are "shut up" under sin only so all might receive the promise of salvation by faith (Galatians 3:22).

Through the gospel, our perfection is found in Christ and not ourselves, eradicating the corrupting influence of pride. What man can boast of what he did not do? What woman can glory in what she was powerless to achieve?

There is no need to compare ourselves to others or to measure ourselves by their standards. Like Abraham, the Lord calls us only to *believe* (John 6:29). Then, as our faith matures, we can experience the fuller measures of the love and grace that God has destined for us.

CIRCUMCISED HEARTS

Water baptism is a *covenant ceremony* in which a person publicly enters into the new covenant, dying to the old individualistic life and being raised into a new life in Christ. "Passing through the water and being buried" also relates to the heart being circumcised:

> And in Him you were also circumcised with a circumcision made without hands, in the removal of the body of the flesh by the circumcision of Christ; having been buried with Him in baptism, in which you were also raised up with Him through faith in the working of God, who raised Him from the dead. When you were dead in your transgressions and the uncircumcision of your flesh, He made you alive together

with Him, having forgiven us all our transgressions, having canceled out the certificate of debt consisting of decrees [*dogma*] against us, which was hostile to us; and He has taken it out of the way, having nailed it to the cross. Colossians 2:11–14

The "certificate of debt" is the debt to perfection that we owe in our quest to be like God. Paul is saying that our debt has been nailed to the cross and declared, "Paid in full!" When we are baptized into Christ, we are freed from the need to meet unattainable standards. Our "creditors" might continue to harass us, but they do so without legal grounds.

Equally important, when we accept Jesus by faith into our lives, we allow our hearts to become "circumcised." God begins "cutting away" our old sinful nature, right from our core. This disarming of sin is what propels us into freedom. Humanity does not need more laws to modify our behavior, but rather a circumcision of the heart in which God replaces our old, sinful hearts of stone with new, tender hearts of flesh. These are new, holy hearts—cleansed by the blood of Jesus—in which His presence dwells, and on which His laws are written:

> "Moreover, I will give you a new heart and put a new spirit within you; and I will remove the heart of stone from your flesh and give you a heart of flesh. I will put My Spirit within you and cause you to walk in My statutes, and you will be careful to observe My ordinances. You will live in the land that I gave to your forefathers; so you will be My people, and I will be your God." Ezekiel 36:26–28

It was through Abraham's physical circumcision that new life was miraculously imparted for the birth of Isaac and the vast nation that followed. And it is through circumcised hearts that the vigor of spiritual life is miraculously imparted to God's people. The awesome result is multiplied blessings being extended to all the families of the earth.

THE ESSENCE OF CHRISTIANITY

How do we define freedom? Some would say that freedom is the ability to do anything we want, but such selfish living leads only to further bondage. From a Biblical perspective, freedom means being delivered from the Adamic curse, thriving without imposed standards for righteousness, and reigning over our internal passions.

It is a sad commentary of our ignorance that we often equate Biblical living with rules and requirements rather than freedom. In Christ, we are free from having to measure up, free from having to meet the exacting requirements of human and divine standards in order to be embraced as acceptable and approved.

Jesus died as both a transgressor of the law and a covenant breaker—the Passover Lamb sacrificed for the forgiveness of our sins. Our debt to perfection was nailed to His cross, forever freeing us from the compulsion to measure up. God also gives us new hearts and empowers us to live differently through the vitality of grace. Because of this, we can move from a "fear of" to a "desire to" motivation.

Humanity was created to be free in the garden of Eden, and it is to freedom that our souls long to return. We can find some common ground between the various religions, but they all involve meeting standards for acceptance or exaltation. Christianity is different; no other system of belief offers the depth of freedom that we find and experience through the new covenant gospel of grace.

> Stand fast therefore in the liberty by which Christ has made us free, and do not be entangled again with a yoke of bondage. Indeed I, Paul, say to you that if you become circumcised, Christ will profit you nothing. And I testify again to every man who becomes circumcised that he is a debtor to keep the whole law. You have become estranged from Christ, you who attempt to be justified by law; you have fallen from grace. For we through the Spirit eagerly wait for the hope of righteousness by faith. For in Christ Jesus neither

circumcision nor uncircumcision avails anything, but faith working through love. Galatians 5:1–6 (NKJV)

What a challenging and powerful passage! True life is not about obeying or abandoning standards of law. The heart of spiritual vitality centers on living out the simplicity of God's design: *faith working through love*, or *faith expressing itself through love*. Of course, there are those who will want to make life more complicated with all sorts of requirements, but the gospel really is that simple.

Do you remember the two virtues that characterize God's covenants? *Faith* and *love* are the New Testament expressions of *faithfulness* and *lovingkindness*. In Biblical thought, the line between faith and faithfulness is nearly imperceptible.[5] A heart of faith produces a life of faithfulness. The essence of life, it turns out, is the essence of covenantal living. It is through faith that we enter into a sacred co-union with God, and it is out of faith that the rich fruit of faithful love grows.

Again, with the new covenant gospel, the burden of perfection falls upon Jesus and not upon us. This means that, while we are to grow in faith and love, we need not be perfect. There is no dogma thrust upon us to say that our faith and love must meet certain standards. Instead, empowered by the Holy Spirit and firmly established through grace as the covenant children of God, we can grow in trust and love from the inside out.

The cross is problematic only in that it presents a stumbling block to the self-righteous by declaring our inherent unworthiness. Without standards of righteousness, there is no stairway to heaven for people to climb, and thus, no reason to boast. This returns us to a state of dependence upon God and destroys the quest for self-glorification.

It is by faith that we "appropriate" Christ's work on the cross for our lives. The process is somewhat like receiving a gift card. That card

---

5. Rudolf Bultmann, "Πιστεύω, Πίστις, Πιστός, Πιστόω, Ἄπιστος, Ἀπιστέω, Ἀπιστία, Ὀλιγόπιστος, Ὀλιγοπιστία," ed. Gerhard Kittel, Geoffrey W. Bromiley, and Gerhard Friedrich, *Theological Dictionary of the New Testament* (Grand Rapids, MI: Eerdmans, 1964), 199.

has value, but it does us no good until we appropriate it at the store. Christ died for all, but we apply His sacrifice to our lives by believing and entering into a new covenant relationship with Him.

We are saved by grace through faith, with love being the resulting fruit. Love, then, leads us to do good works *in response* to God's love for us. Our good works have no power to save us, but they do serve as indicators of a living and growing faith. Under the new covenant, the *law of love* is the driving force that governs our lives.

In a law-based world, people are bound by the fear of sinning. *If the gospel of Christ binds us to anything, it is the voluntary choice to love.*

> For the love of Christ controls us, having concluded this, that one died for all, therefore all died; and He died for all, so that they who live might no longer live for themselves, but for Him who died and rose again on their behalf. 2 Corinthians 5:14–15

The Greek word translated as "controls" in 2 Corinthians 5:14 can mean to hold a person fast—as of a prisoner—or to force into a narrow channel—as a strait would do to a ship.[6]

Imagine yourself as a teenage male. (Unless you are a teenage male. Then you can just imagine you as yourself.) Something within you loves to speed—especially when you see speed limit signs. In your dream world, you would travel ten times the speed of any sign with no adverse consequences. After innumerable tickets, you find yourself once again standing before Judge Williams. Expecting the gavel to come down hard, you nervously await a harsh sentence from this stern-looking man. After all, you deserve it. The judge, however, catches you off guard.

"Young man, I am going to declare you to be free of all speed limit laws. I am instructing the police officers in our community to give you a free pass. You can go as fast as you like."

---

6. James Strong, *Enhanced Strong's Lexicon* (Woodside Bible Fellowship, 1995).

Nearly overcome with excitement, you begin to think about an amazing life of speed-filled freedom.

"There is one catch," the judge adds. "I want you to spend a morning with me before I send you on your way."

The judge's stipulation seems reasonable and more than worth the effort, so you readily agree. Before long, you and Judge Williams are stopping at a cemetery. There, you see a tombstone that reads, "Joey Williams, killed by a speeding driver at age six." Unnerved a little, you begin to fidget. The judge says nothing.

Your next stop is a hospital. Judge Williams gives the nurses a nod, and they allow you both to enter the pediatric intensive care unit. There, through a window, you see a little girl, her face swollen and bruised with tubes running to several machines. Beside her are a man, woman, and two other children weeping uncontrollably. The little girl is brain-dead, and they are about to pull the plug. A quick memory of a recent newscast flashes through your mind. A speeding driver lost control of his car and hit the girl as she was playing jump rope on the sidewalk. Now, she, too, is leaving this world at a tender age, and her family will be immersed in grief for many days to come.

Not a sound comes from the judge's lips, but as you wipe a tear from your eye, you both know he has made his point. Staying true to his word, Judge Williams then gives you a "free to speed" card that you can show to police officers when you get pulled over for breaking the limit. That card, however, will no longer be necessary.

Driving through town on the way to a friend's house, you see that nothing about the route has changed. The same speed limit signs sit in the same places. But *you* have changed. Not wanting to bring grief to another family by your selfish actions, you voluntarily drive at a safe speed. Free to do as you will, you are now bound by love.

BOND-SERVANTS

When we enter into a new covenant relationship with God, we voluntarily bind ourselves to His will. The apostle Paul even went so far as to call himself a "bond-servant" of God (see Romans 1:1). God's will is for us to trust and to love in all that we do. It is a deep love for Christ that "shackles" us to His plans and purposes. We are free to do as we want, but what we want is to bless and honor our Lord in every possible way.

When we think about who He is, how much He loves us, and the extreme sacrifice that He made on our behalf, what else can we do but love Him wholeheartedly in return? If our Christian path seems to be narrower than that of our culture, it is only because we have chosen to surrender our freedoms so that we might glorify the Lord in all things.

This line of thinking brings us full circle. In the garden, all God really wanted was for humanity to live in love. We experience a taste of paradise when we love freely and faithfully. A husband and wife devoted to one another through the ups and downs of life. A person freed from the weight of sin and burdensome expectations. A church family experiencing the joy of rich relationships through meaningful service. All are but tastes of the love paradigm that characterizes God's kingdom.

> Owe nothing to anyone except to love one another; for he who loves his neighbor has fulfilled the law. For this, "You shall not commit adultery, You shall not murder, You shall not steal, You shall not covet," and if there is any other commandment, it is summed up in this saying, "You shall love your neighbor as yourself." Love does no wrong to a neighbor; therefore love is the fulfillment of the law. Romans 13:8–10

From the Lord's perspective, our human existence has always been about love and never about rules. Christian living is not characterized by an "I have to" motivation, but rather one of "I want to." God does not give us long lists of rules to follow and scores of obligations to meet. Instead, He circumcises our hearts so He can write His laws upon them. The Christian's life, then, is governed from the inside out.

Our touch of paradise grows stronger as we mature in our love. No longer is our joy limited to fleeting feelings of pleasure that come from desires fulfilled, but rather we begin to draw from a deep well of significance and assurance that is rooted in covenant love. We, then, will carry this mature and free love with us into the everlasting paradise that we call "heaven." In heaven, we will experience all the richness of the new covenant as we are eternally wed to Christ. On that day, God will put on a banquet that will make even the greatest human feast seem like a week-old deli sandwich—green meat and all.

Heaven does not have to wait—at least not entirely. By understanding and living out the essence of the new covenant—*faith expressing itself through love*—we can help bring the life-giving kingdom of heaven to earth.

Now, as appealing as the essence of the gospel might be, drinking its truth can also be unpleasant. In a Biblical context, faith and love are both *covenant* concepts—meaning that their exercise apart from a relationship with God has little meaning in heaven's eyes. In other words, humans do not have the authority to determine what faith and love should look like as they play out on a day-to-day basis. The God who designed and initiated the new covenant is the *only* One who has the right to determine all that is good.

In our day, there exists a dangerous—and even deadly—universalism which reasons that because God is love, He will never condemn anyone to hell. That reasoning, however, stems from a human logic that fails to regard the blessing-curse mindset innate to Biblical covenants. Yes, God's door to salvation stands open wide for all who seek to enter through faith in Christ. However, those who do not appropriate the blood of the eternal Passover Lamb to the "doorposts" of their lives, remain, by default, under the Adamic curse.

Only the Creator of humanity has the right to define the true nature of faith and love. *We must trust and love according to God's design.* Anything else is either idolatry or humanism—both products of earthly logic. The pursuit of wisdom is also vital because we do not always know what faith and love should look like in a given situation.

We cannot tell God's river of wisdom where to go; we can only follow where it leads.[7] Ever so thankfully, the Lord's wisdom always leads us to the land of freedom.

WRAP-UP

Freely, we enter into a new covenant relationship with God, and freely, we abide in His love as we are transformed from the inside out. It is not about the "have to" but about the "want to" that comes as a result of being given new hearts of flesh in exchange for our old hearts of stone.

The gospel of Christ frees us from the burdensome requirements of the law and returns us to the simplicity of Eden, but in a far better capacity. To trust and to love are Christ's primary commandments, and they find their expression as we rest in the security and simplicity of the new covenant.

DISCUSSION

1. What can make the knowledge of good just as deadly as the knowledge of evil?
2. How is the human conscience similar to the Mosaic law?
3. Explain cultural legalism, and give a contemporary example.
4. What is the essence of new covenant living as found in Galatians 5:6?
5. Why do we need God's wisdom to live out this essence?
6. What does it mean to be "bound by love"?

---

7. Santos, *Say Goodbye to Regret*, 221.

Chapter Eleven

THE PREVAILING CHURCH

"Upon this rock I will build My church; and the gates of Hades will not overpower it."

Matthew 16:18b

One hundred religious persons knit into a unity by careful organizations do not constitute a church any more than eleven dead men make a football team. The first requisite is life, always.

—A. W. Tozer

For my first job out of college, I had to drive south about twenty minutes to a laboratory that was adjacent to a local power plant. Along the road was an old barn painted with a sign on the side that read, "Take your family to church." The idea of encouraging parents to take their kids to church might seem to some people like a good one, but sadly, that billboard message assumed an ideal world that does not exist. Let us briefly explore the concept of the church.

If I asked you to define the word *church*, how would you answer? To some, the church is a building. To others, it is an institution. From a Biblical perspective, however, the church is more like an *organism*—a living, breathing entity made up of numerous parts. And specifically, *people* are those parts. The church is the *body of Christ*—the earthly representation of our eternal Savior, made up of human beings.

The concept of the church is multifaceted and carries different meanings for different people. Focusing on the idea that the church is made up of people, we can make a distinction between Christ's "living" church and the human-made "institutional" church. While the living church requires active leadership and organization, the institutional church is characterized by political maneuvering, an unbending structure, and an elitist hierarchy. The institutional church presents a form of religion, but lacks the true life of God. All too often, Christ's church is unjustly blamed for the failings of the institutional church.

With the living church, we find three primary expressions: *a local fellowship, the church in a community,* and *the church universal.* A local fellowship consists of a specific congregation. The church in a community speaks of all Christians in that community—of which the various "churches" are simply different extensions of the same body. The church universal refers to all true Christians worldwide.

While people often focus on outward issues such as the order of worship, dress, and music style, it is the presence—or absence—of God's life and vitality that matters most. A church—and thus the people within—can be active, and even generous, but out of alignment with God's design, devoid of true spiritual life.

What are some indicators of a lifeless church? Prayerlessness, a judgmental environment, infighting, and political posturing are a few. There are multiple reasons why a church can be out of alignment, but three are prevalent:

- Legalism – While there is no one secret to vibrant Christian living, a revelation of grace is central to the Christian experience. When lists of rules and external requirements characterize a church, not only will it be lifeless, it will stifle the true spiritual life of God. These organizations might emphasize the importance of the Bible but leave little room for the Holy Spirit to work in their midst.

I have taught small group Bible studies for over thirty years, and I cannot begin to tell you how many people came to those groups struggling with their Christian beliefs because of their childhood experiences in legalistic families and churches. It is heartbreaking when people who profess Jesus as Lord and Savior lack an understanding of the spiritual freedom for which He died. Strict adherence to the letter of the law will have the very opposite of its intended effect. It is the Spirit of God who brings life.

- Humanism – The other end of the spectrum is "religious humanism," in which Biblical integrity matters little, and the focus becomes human-centered. Without holding to the Bible as the inspired, infallible, and authoritative Word of God, we are inclined to impose human ideals into religious settings. In this type of environment, grace is often viewed as a license to do as one wants, rather than an empowering force from God that enables us to live according to His design.[1]

- A Celebrity Culture – As Christians, our identity is based upon our *relationship* with God, not on any number of external factors.[2] This is a key point of the gospel that is often neglected or misunderstood. The unfortunate result is a quest for human glory that spawns a celebrity culture in which "elite" leaders are lauded with special titles, honors, and wealth. Celebrity-driven churches tend to build their own kingdoms in the name of God's glory. Image becomes tantamount even as internal decay scars and damages lives. I am not suggesting that we dishonor our leaders, but that the true heart of Christian leadership is rooted in humble servanthood.

When we contemplate the character of God, the sin, death, and destruction of our world can easily darken our vision. Something

---

1. Bob Santos, *The Divine Progression of Grace: Blazing a Trail to Fruitful Living* (Indiana, PA: SfMe Media, 2014).
2. Bob Santos, *From Glory to Glory: Finding Real Significance in an Image-Driven World* (Indiana, PA: SfMe Media, 2018).

similar applies to the church, and maybe more so. Our perspective of Christ's church is further convoluted by the errant theology and human brokenness that often plague our congregations. I am not trying to minimize the bad behavior that we see from Christians; I am trying to establish a perspective that aligns with the Scriptures.

Despite our struggles to live out the Christian faith, the Bible tells us that Jesus loves the church and will one day return for her as His "bride" without spot or blemish (Ephesians 5:25–33). *If we truly love the Lord, we will want to understand the nature of the church and respond in a way that resonates with His love.*

At a relatively young age, I was elected to the "elder" board at our church. I jumped in with a vision of all that we could do together for the gospel. What a massive disappointment! Immaturity among longtime members made it virtually impossible to make any significant progress. Rather than effectively advancing the cause of Christ, we instead kept an almost continual inward focus because of the unnecessary drama that immaturity brings.

Serving six years on that board—during which time I experienced up close the underbelly of the local church—had a profound effect on me. The people blamed the leaders for all manner of problems, while the leaders blamed the people for being unwilling to grow and serve. I also began to realize that the flaws so prevalent in our small local fellowship (which has changed considerably since) were characteristic of the Western church as a whole.

Knowing of Christ's deep love for the church, I decided that I would not become a church antagonist, but rather spend my life building her up. So when my final term on the board came to an end, Debi and I began serving in college ministry with a vision to help reach and train future church leaders and laborers. After seeing a large number of our students go on to serve in a variety of church capacities, we launched Search for Me Ministries to help form and equip a generation of world changers for Christ. The underlying goal of our ministry efforts has always involved enabling Christians to grow toward spiritual maturity for the sake of the local church.

OUR COVENANT UNITY IN CHRIST

Throughout this book, I have emphasized that Jesus is our covenant representative—that He alone was worthy to enter into a sacred covenant with the heavenly Father on behalf of humanity. Because of His actions, any person can be in a covenant with the Creator of all things. Now, please allow me to present this truth with a slightly different emphasis: Jesus Christ is *our* covenant representative. What am I saying?

All who enter into the new covenant in Christ also enter into a sacred and binding relationship with one another. It is this group of reborn people who constitute the living church, the body of Christ. The ramifications are significant! We truly are brothers and sisters in the Lord, regardless of race, ethnicity, or nationality. And according to the Scriptures, this spiritual family of God is the highest order of family known to humanity (see Matthew 12:46-50).

After a particularly challenging encounter with a rich young ruler, Peter blurted out to Jesus, "We've given up everything to follow you" (Mark 10:28, NLT). Jesus responded with a statement that is sometimes misunderstood:

> "I assure you that everyone who has given up house or brothers or sisters or mother or father or children or property, for my sake and for the Good News, will receive now in return a hundred times as many houses, brothers, sisters, mothers, children, and property—along with persecution. And in the world to come that person will have eternal life."
> Mark 10:29b-30 (NLT)

In spite of what some television preachers might tell us, Jesus was not promising us material wealth by multiplying all we sacrifice by exactly one hundred. Rather, He was proclaiming that God will meet our every need through the covenant body of Christ. Those who make extreme sacrifices—including being ostracized by their biological families—can find great comfort in this passage. *None of us are alone in this world; we are all part of the immense covenant family of God that spreads across the globe.*

This perspective of the covenant body of Christ creates some obvious issues—the most significant question involves who is truly a Christian and who is simply putting on a show. We are left with an abundance of loose ends that do not seem to bother God—at least for now (see Matthew 13:24–30). The time will come when the Lord makes all things clear, but for today, we are called to wisely walk in love and preserve our covenant unity in Christ:

> Therefore I, the prisoner of the Lord, implore you to walk in a manner worthy of the calling with which you have been called, with all humility and gentleness, with patience, showing tolerance for one another in love, being diligent to preserve the unity of the Spirit in the bond of peace. There is one body and one Spirit, just as also you were called in one hope of your calling; one Lord, one faith, one baptism, one God and Father of all who is over all and through all and in all. Ephesians 4:1–6

I feel as though we too quickly dismiss passages such as this. And while there will be times when we have just reason to disagree with other professing Christians, it is vital that we align our attitudes with God's design. We begin by first realizing how much Christian unity matters to God. Just before going to the cross, Jesus prayed:

> "I do not ask on behalf of these alone, but for those also who believe in Me through their word; that they may all be one; even as You, Father, are in Me and I in You, that they also may be in Us, so that the world may believe that You sent Me.

> "The glory which You have given Me I have given to them, that they may be one, just as We are one; I in them and You in Me, that they may be perfected in unity, so that the world may know that You sent Me, and loved them, even as You have loved Me." John 17:20–23

Wow! Did you catch the significance of this passage? *The Lord longs for His children, in all of their diversity, to live in unity.* And if we truly love Him, we will value what He values.

The idea of a unified church might seem impossible to some, but would the Son of God lift a request to the Father that had no possibility of being answered? I think not. Furthermore, would the heavenly Father be willing and able to answer such an audacious request? Of course, He would. Perhaps ours is the era in which Christians will finally take our Savior's full desires to heart.

The unity of Christ's body is near the top of God's "Christmas wish list," and right there with it is the *witness* that our unity presents to the unsaved. At least in part, the Western church has lost cultural influence because we have largely failed to love one another and live out the covenant unity that God commands.

The devil, it seems, has taken more heed to the words of Christ than has the church.

> "If a kingdom is divided against itself, that kingdom cannot stand. If a house is divided against itself, that house will not be able to stand." Mark 3:24–25

Hell delights in dividing and conquering, and we too easily fall prey to its dark schemes. Too easily we judge, too quickly we condemn, and too brazenly we criticize—all while ignoring the precious words of Scripture that we claim to honor. Jesus is not just calling us to a feigned peace; He is calling us to love one another with the same gracious love that He extends to us.

> "A new commandment I give to you, that you love one another, even as I have loved you, that you also love one another. By this all men will know that you are My disciples, if you have love for one another." John 13:34–35

We honor our covenant with God by treating our fellow Christians with love, honor, and respect. We dishonor Him when we look down upon other believers with callous condescension because of our supposedly superior beliefs. And in doing so, we not only disregard one of the commands closest to our Savior's heart, we also further alienate the unsaved. Why has the Western church lost so much cultural influence? We have squandered a precious opportunity by failing to love one another as our Lord commands.

In contrast, something near-mystical occurs when God's people come together as one. Through covenant unity, we experience an impartation of divine life and the manifestation of true glory. It is a life-giving power that cannot be contained and cannot help but spill into the dying world around us. We do not need to create this unity; we only need to preserve the covenant oneness that we *already* have in Christ. Nor do we need to cut covenants, like in the Old Testament, with our Christian friends. This lasting, beautiful familial covenant already exists between us, and we remind ourselves of it every time we partake in communion together.

We must also remember the difference between *unity* and *uniformity*. A uniform oneness compels everyone to follow the same script of appearance, belief, and organizational practice. On the contrary, true unity centers on our oneness in Christ through the new covenant. Our theologies need not be identical on every point. Nor should organizations give up their individual distinctions in order to get along. *When we embrace our covenant oneness with each other, we simply declare that there is one issue—the full embrace of Jesus Christ as our Lord and Savior—that prevails above all others.*

Not long after I began working in college ministry, the Lord laid bare my selfish motives. That profound experience opened my eyes and instilled within me a "kingdom mindset." We soon began working with other campus fellowships. Later, after Debi and I started Search for Me Ministries, we began using our building to host campus minister luncheons and prayer meetings. More recently, I have become actively involved with a pastor's network in our community.

Through these deliberate and persistent efforts to preserve the unity that we have in Christ, we are seeing the Lord work in dynamic ways. In addition to the many individual and group testimonies that we hear about the working of the Holy Spirit, the overall "spiritual temperature" of our community continues to rise. In the process, everyone but the devil benefits. It is not until ministry leaders finally let go of control and stop building their own kingdoms that the Lord begins to answer prayers for their community in earnest.

Finally, while our unity is in Christ, it is not unity at all costs. There will always be charlatans who pose as Christians, humanists who seek to impose personal ideologies, and genuine Christians who have character and doctrinal issues that need to be addressed. That is why we are called to *love* as Christ loves—patiently, sacrificially, and wisely.

Covenant love calls us to challenge, correct, and confront our brothers and sisters who are going off course. The manner in which we do this, however, means everything. We begin with private and humble—but firm—communication (see Matthew 18:15-17; Galatians 6:1). If the individual refuses to respond, we escalate our efforts by incorporating an increasingly larger sphere. From my experience, far too many Christians either refuse to confront, or they do so unwisely, with arrogance and without respect.

THE LOCAL BODY

The idea of covenant oneness can sound appealing in principle, but we are not just talking about vague concepts. Love is not a nebulous feeling to pass on from a distance—similar to liking a social media post—but rather practical action expressed in real relationships. Substantive relationships cannot be sustained from afar—at least not for very long. God builds us together, side by side, in a local context.

> And coming to Him as to a living stone which has been rejected by men, but is choice and precious in the sight of God, you also, as living stones, are being built up as a spiritual house for a holy priesthood, to offer up spiritual sacrifices acceptable to God through Jesus Christ. 1 Peter 2:4-5

The church is a body of believers crafted together by the Holy Spirit, with *love* being the *glue* that holds the stones in place (Colossians 3:14). Anyone who has ever worked with people understands how difficult it can be for individuals with diverse preferences, desires, and opinions to get along. *When God's people willingly work through the personal biases, self-centered attitudes, and hurt feelings that accompany any genuine relationship, heaven smiles with delight.*

The church is central to New Testament theology, and the idea that a person can have a vibrant walk with God without being connected to a local body of believers has no Biblical foundation. It is in a local body that we learn, grow, and mature. The local church also serves as the primary vehicle by which God's kingdom is advanced on this earth. Parachurch ministries can play an important role in outreach and discipleship, but only as they serve the church.

This emphasis on the importance of the local church brings me back to that old "Take your family to church" barn sign and the realization that not all churches are good for our spiritual well-being. How, then, do we choose where to connect?

In addition to understanding the concepts mentioned above, we can ask a few key questions that will help narrow our choices:

- Does this church consider the Bible to be the inspired, infallible, and authoritative Word of God? Communication from heaven is central to the church's mission and purpose, indeed, its very existence. The church is not merely a social club or activist organization. It is the body of Christ, and the Bible declares Jesus to be the Word of God (John 1:1).

- Is this church healthy? Do not look for perfection among the leaders; look for spiritual and emotional health. Are they humble, transparent, and noncontrolling? If a local fellowship is healthy, you can work through any problems that arise.

- Is this church outwardly focused? A healthy Christian body believes strongly in the importance of reaching outside of itself. If a group of professing believers is simply "holding down the fort" and condemning all that is outside its walls, they are missing the true heart of God.

I also encourage people to seek the Lord for guidance on *where* He wants to plant them. Debi and I have been in the same church for over thirty-five years. During those years, we have had to work through some terribly painful struggles. There were times when we would have been well-justified in leaving, but we stayed because we felt that God wanted us to be there.

Before we joined our current church, we attended a local fellowship that seemed to have a high degree of spirituality. We had every intention of becoming members until a series of events caused us to question our course of action. Debi and I eventually left, but we did so graciously. In retrospect, it is now obvious that the Lord had a better fit for us. We still have many good friends in that congregation and often work together for the cause of the gospel.

At first glance, leaving a church might seem like a violation of covenant faithfulness—as though we are getting divorced and breaking a sacred bond. This need not be the case, however. When my wife and I got married, we exchanged vows with *each other*. When I was water baptized, however, I was baptized into *the church of Jesus Christ*—not a specific fellowship or denomination. Our covenant commitment is to Jesus and to the body of Christ as a whole. Yes, we want to get firmly and faithfully established in a local fellowship, but we also need to understand how we fit into His greater body.

The seasons of life bring changes, and churches that were once thriving and vibrant might find themselves stuck in old, unfruitful ways. New leadership might take a church in a different direction. Or perhaps a personal situation changes. A new spouse, the birth of a child, and a new work schedule might all be valid reasons for us moving to a different local fellowship. I am not suggesting that we get into the habit of "church hopping" every time we feel a bit of discomfort, but rather that we seek the Lord to find the place where we fit best on the local level. Trying to force ourselves into a church where we are not called can cause frustration levels to skyrocket for everyone involved.

The decision to stay or leave is one that only you can make. If others are pressuring or trying to manipulate you, something is not healthy. Neither is it healthy to allow discontentment with a church to simmer and stew. The best route is to squarely face your issues and prayerfully chart a course of action to deal with them.

If you decide a church change is necessary, please do everything with a kingdom mindset by seeking the well-being of all involved. If you are leaving because of a church problem that will not be remedied soon, be careful of a "knee-jerk reaction" and creating unnecessary damage when leaving. Communicate well with the church leaders, and avoid "burning bridges." We do not know what the future holds.

GROWING TO MATURITY

Church attendance is unfulfilling for many people because they approach it with a "What's in it for me?" consumer mentality. The result is the all-too-common problem of a few hard workers wearing themselves out doing the majority of the labor. But church consumers are missing the heart of true Christian vitality; being blessed is inherently tied to being a blessing to others.

Getting more deeply involved with the life and service of the church also enables us to build some of our closest relationships. Volunteering for the building committee, serving alongside someone in the nursery, or joining a small group can give us an opportunity to get to know one another on a deeper level.

Understanding the wisdom of local church involvement requires that we grasp one of God's primary goals for each of our lives: *becoming mature and fruitful servants in His kingdom*. Calling to mind our previous chapters, "Be fruitful and multiply" were the very first words spoken by God to humanity. Eating from the tree of the knowledge of good and evil then led to a curse of unfruitfulness.

It was for this reason that the Mosaic law fell short; the law failed to make the children of Israel spiritually fruitful. The New Testament, and particularly the gospel of Jesus Christ, brings us back to the goal of becoming fully fruitful believers.

The process of becoming a fully fruitful Christian works best when we are deeply planted in the growth-oriented environment of a healthy local church. It is a place where we are given transformational Bible-based instruction, real-life encouragement, and the opportunity to serve according to the gifts that God has given us. The local church is also where our faith and love develop and grow.

If a person has a mind to be critical, any local church will provide plenty of fodder. (If God had a mind to be critical, how much could He find wrong in your life?) We are talking about an organization of imperfect people—all at various stages of maturity. Problems are inevitable. Even the New Testament church that many Christians seem to idolize had its share of issues. The Corinthians, for example, struggled with factions caused by a celebrity culture, worked through the problem of incest among its members, and were forced to address the issue of people getting drunk at their church fellowship dinners. Human lives are messy, and church life often puts us on the front lines of the human condition as the Lord seeks to redeem and transform our lives on every level.

Growing together as a temple of living stones is never a neat, tidy process. When we work closely together as the body of Christ, our frail humanity cannot help but rise to the surface. We might have to deal with differences of perspective or communication breakdowns. Sometimes, our natural selfishness simply rears its ugly head. But it is through this process of highs and lows, the pleasant and the difficult, that the growth of maturity is intended to take place. Unfortunately, some people bail out at the hint of conflict—short-circuiting the growth process before it has the opportunity to run its course.

Even in a healthy relationship, personal hurts are unavoidable. Life cannot be otherwise. In this world, we relate to imperfect people, and you are one of them. If we are growing toward maturity, however, we will learn how to fully forgive those who offend us, how to work through our issues, and how to have healthy discussions. In the security of the new covenant, we can work out the love of God in practical ways and without the fear of being abandoned.

Assuming that a church environment is basically healthy (and not manipulative or abusive), the following are three growth concepts that people often overlook, ignore, or misunderstand:

1. Discipline related to growth does not always feel good. The process of child-rearing teaches us this principle. Parents generally know better than children do, and there will be times when parental discipline does not make sense to the child. Along a similar vein, there will be times when it seems as though church leaders—and even God—are out to get us. A good church leader will not strive for popularity, but will make decisions that are best for the people—even when they respond negatively. If being liked and popular is the goal, a job on a cruise ship or ice cream truck might be preferable.

2. The Bible distinguishes between *righteous* and *unrighteous* judgments. It was Jesus Himself who said, "Do not judge according to appearance, but judge with righteous judgment" (John 7:24). While a judgmental environment fails to reflect the love of God, there are times when we are called to make righteous judgments.

    How do we distinguish between judgments that are righteous and those that are unrighteous? A righteous judgment honestly assesses a situation in light of Scriptural truth and has a redemptive goal in mind. Unrighteous judgments are driven by selfish agendas—such as looking down on someone so that we can feel better about ourselves. Unrighteous judgments usually seek to exalt one person above another, with a sense of permanence, no less. On the contrary, righteous judgments are redemptive; they seek the best for all and carry a sense of hope for a better future.

Let us say, for example, that a young cohabitating couple begins attending a local church. As they get more involved, the pastor pulls them aside and explains the importance of the marriage covenant and the sinfulness of a sexual relationship outside of marriage. To the couple, it can seem as though they are being judged, belittled, and rejected when, in reality, the pastor cares enough to risk their displeasure. Please do not allow hurt feelings to cloud your vision; to be righteously judged is to be loved.

3. Treating one another with honor and respect is central to Christian living. To some, this seems like an obvious statement, but in light of social media toxicity, it might present a radical departure from common practice.

   Do you remember God's statement to Abraham from Genesis 12:3? "Him who dishonors you I will curse." The Lord extends *hesed* toward His covenant children, wrath toward those who have not repented of their human rebellion, and absolute fury toward those who mistreat His royal sons and daughters. But what happens when genuine Christians—who are covenant members of Christ's body—dishonor one another? If God has your back because you are His child, He also has mine. To dishonor one another, *at the very minimum*, is to misalign with God's design, creating dysfunction within His body and damaging ourselves. (Please read 1 Corinthians 11:17–34.)

Few churches are what they should be. Such is our human reality. But how do we respond? Do we become scoffers who tear down, or servants of Christ who seek to build up? Are our views being shaped by the Bible or by cultural forces that hate God and His people?

EDIFICATION

The apostle Paul reminds us that the basic motivation behind all that we do is to be *edification*. Immediately after exhorting the Ephesian church to "preserve the unity of the Spirit in the bond of peace," Paul penned the following:

> And He gave some as apostles, and some as prophets, and some as evangelists, and some as pastors and teachers, for the equipping of the saints for the work of service, to the building up of the body of Christ; until we all attain to the unity of the faith, and of the knowledge of the Son of God, to a mature man, to the measure of the stature which belongs to the fullness of Christ. As a result, we are no longer to be children, tossed here and there by waves and carried about by every wind of doctrine, by the trickery of men, by craftiness in deceitful scheming; but speaking the truth in love, we are to grow up in all aspects into Him who is the head, even Christ, from whom the whole body, being fitted and held together by what every joint supplies, according to the proper working of each individual part, causes the growth of the body for the building up of itself in love. Ephesians 4:11–16

This passage provides a basic template for local church function, whereby we seek to build up the body of Christ. And as we work through conflicts and issues together, we all grow toward maturity. Perhaps even more importantly, we develop a synergy through which we can accomplish more together than we ever could apart.

In no way do I believe that the church's issues are beyond hope. After all, Jesus has a history of transforming even the vilest of sinners. In addition to faith and love, I believe that wisdom is our greatest need. Yes, we often seek to learn how to operate our churches better, but what we lack is a deeper understanding of how to bring people into a fully fruitful Christian lifestyle. *Creative techniques can help us draw a crowd, but it takes wisdom to disciple people to maturity.*

I am not blind to the dysfunction that exists in many Christian churches. At the same time, I recognize God's passion and want to serve His desires to the best of my ability. Moses' story is not within the context of the local church, but it inspires me nonetheless:

> By faith Moses, when he had grown up, refused to be called the son of Pharaoh's daughter, choosing rather to endure ill-treatment with the people of God than to enjoy the passing pleasures of sin, considering the reproach of Christ greater riches than the treasures of Egypt; for he was looking to the reward. Hebrews 11:24-26

Moses saw something that so many people miss! He had the treasures of Egypt at his fingertips but sought the greater eternal blessing of serving God's people—even when they mistreated him. Moses chose to be a builder rather than a scoffer. What about us? What will we do?

The Bible teaches that the church is a body and that we are all parts of one another (1 Corinthians 12:12-27). And what do we call it when a body attacks itself? An autoimmune disease. When we unrighteously judge, criticize, and belittle other Christians, in a very real sense, we attack ourselves—with painful results.

I have read 1 Corinthians 12 more times than I can count, but during my last time through, a single verse captivated my attention:

> And if one member suffers, all the members suffer with it;
> if one member is honored, all the members rejoice with it.
> 1 Corinthians 12:26

At that moment, I realized that I rarely rejoice when prominent Christian leaders—the ones who have the gifts, status, and success that I wish I had—are honored. I determined to change my attitude and begin celebrating their successes. In doing so, I feel as though I benefitted the most. In blessing, we are blessed.

WRAP-UP

Why treat other Christians with honor and respect even when they appear unworthy? Why pray blessings when we are tempted to complain? Why forgive when we are hurt or offended? Why stay connected to a local fellowship even when it feels bad? It is because we are bound by a deep love for the head of the church—our Lord and Savior Jesus Christ. The church is God's idea, and He loves her with all of His heart. The idea of a vibrant Christian life apart from local involvement conflicts with Biblical teaching at its very roots.

It does not matter what failures we have seen in the past. Nor can we use the lifeless form of the institutional church as an excuse for avoiding involvement on the local level. Jesus will fill this earth with His life-giving kingdom, and He will do it through His beloved church—through *His people*, not through mere buildings or programs.

In these last days, our God is doing yet another amazing work: *He is uniting His people in covenant oneness.* The world has yet to see and experience a unified church that is fully bound together by the covenant love of God. Only a unified church can thrive while swimming against the cultural tides of persecution, control, and obstruction of truth. A single fellowship can positively influence a community, but it takes the collective body of Christ to bring lasting transformation.[3] In the end, not only will the church survive, by God's grace, she will prevail over darkness. Oh, how our planet needs a prevailing church!

DISCUSSION

1. Why is it important to get involved with a healthy church and not just any church?
2. What are some indicators of a healthy church?
3. How does faithful involvement with a local church help us grow toward maturity?
4. How does unity differ from uniformity?
5. What is the basis for our Christian unity?
6. What singular motivation should cause us to celebrate and preserve the unity of the church?

---

3. Bob Santos, *Community Prayer Devotional* (Indiana, PA: SfMe Media, 2019).

Chapter Twelve

LIVING OUT THE NEW COVENANT

Therefore, my beloved brethren, be steadfast, immovable, always abounding in the work of the Lord, knowing that your toil is not in vain in the Lord.

1 Corinthians 15:58

All of God's people are ordinary people who have been made extraordinary by the purpose he has given them.

—Oswald Chambers

Many brave men and women have walked this planet, but none can compare with Jesus Christ. If ever there was a profile in courage, it was Jesus. To go from being worshiped by all the angels of heaven to hanging naked on a cross—the object of public scorn—is the most extreme transition possible. And He acted willingly.

I want to say that Jesus did all that He did because He loves you and me, but that would be only partly true. During a tense exchange with some of His fellow Jews, the Son of Man said, "If God were your Father, you would love Me, for I proceeded forth and have come from God, for I have not even come on My own initiative, but He sent Me" (John 8:42). The heavenly Father sent Jesus to suffer and die as a sacrifice for our sins. What a profound realization!

Do you remember the story of Mephibosheth from chapter two? Imagine King David relaxing in his royal palace after dinner one evening and saying, "Is there yet anyone left of the house of Saul, that I may show him kindness for Jonathan's sake?" (2 Samuel 9:1). Now picture the Father, Son, and Holy Spirit sitting in the royal courts of heaven, joined by several high-ranking angels. The heavenly Father says, "I have an idea, a plan for something unlike anything We have ever done. I want to create a race of creatures in Our own image, but to make the plan work, One of Us is going to have to suffer horribly."

Immediately, Jesus responds, "I'll do it, Father! I know the price to pay will be steep, but if this is how You want to share Our love, I am all in."

"Go, then, Son. This endeavor will bring both the weight of sin and the fury of hell upon Your head, but it will be worth it in the end."

Now, before you correct my theology and tell me that the Father, Son, and Holy Spirit do not communicate that way, I realize that my ability to describe God's plan is limited. At the same time, this imperfect example helps us better grasp the faithful love and devotion between the Father, Son, and Holy Spirit.

One of the reasons that Jesus lived with such courage is that He came to earth with a love-motivated purpose. The Son of Man knew exactly who He was and what He was about. Human opinion meant nothing; it was the Father's desire that He served.

Christ's courage and purpose were closely intertwined. I doubt that any of His disciples ever said, "Jesus, I triple dog dare you to walk on water!" Something other than a quest for peer approval motivated our Savior. People accept schoolyard dares because they are afraid of public humiliation. Jesus' purpose included public humiliation.

THE BLESSING OF ABRAHAM

Jesus Christ came to earth as the Son of God, but He also came as the Son of Man who took on human form. A humble carpenter fulfilled the destiny that Adam had squandered. I am referring to the Lord's blessing to "Be fruitful and multiply, and fill the earth, and subdue it" (Genesis 1:28). Not only was Christ's life fully fruitful, He also provided the means for us to be fruitful as well.

Jesus is the One who enables us to become fully fruitful, but the process of restoring what Adam had lost began with Abraham:

> "Go forth from your country,
> And from your relatives
> And from your father's house,
> To the land which I will show you;
> And I will make you a great nation,
> And I will bless you,
> And make your name great;
> And so you shall be a blessing;
> And I will bless those who bless you,
> And the one who curses you I will curse.
> And in you all the families of the earth will be blessed."
> Genesis 12:1b–3

God's call to Abraham was based on a *promise*. He was not given the whole plan—only the first step and a basic understanding of the Lord's intent. The divine message was essentially, "Leave your world to become a part of Mine, and you will experience My greatness." The fact that God cut a covenant with Abraham indicated the Lord's intent to be with the man every step of the way.

When we enter into a new covenant relationship with Christ, being delivered from the power of the Adamic curse is only part of the picture. We also inherit Abraham's blessing and the heavenly Father's purposes that accompany it:

> Christ redeemed us from the curse of the Law, having become a curse for us—for it is written, "Cursed is everyone who hangs on a tree"—in order that in Christ Jesus the blessing of Abraham might come to the Gentiles, so that we would receive the promise of the Spirit through faith. Galatians 3:13–14

The Adamic curse was marked by *thorns* and *thistles* polluting the ground, making efforts toward fruitfulness both painful and exhausting (Genesis 3:17-19). Later, when Jesus shared the parable of the sower, it was the seed *among thorns* that proved unfruitful (Matthew 13:7). But Jesus was not talking about the physical ground. Remember, it was spiritual fruitfulness that mattered to the Son of God (Galatians 5:22-23). And on the day that the King of Glory was crucified, Roman soldiers pressed a *crown of thorns* upon His brow (John 19:2). Jesus took upon Himself our curse of unfruitfulness so that the blessing of Abraham might come to us in its fullness.

Jewish tradition tells us that God gave the Mosaic law on the first Feast of the Harvest (i.e., Pentecost). *Three thousand* men died that day because they failed to meet the standard of law presented by the Ten Commandments (Exodus 32:25-28). On the first Feast of the Harvest after Jesus rose from the dead, the Holy Spirit was poured out in the upper room, and *three thousand* souls received a divine impartation of life (Acts 2:1-41).

The outpouring of the Holy Spirit on Pentecost was only the beginning of all that God would do because of Christ's selfless and courageous life. It was Jesus who said, "It is more blessed to give than to receive" (Acts 20:35). In every way possible, His life on earth reflected that statement. So too, through the empowerment of the Spirit, can we fulfill our purposes by blessing those around us.

WATER BAPTISM

We now come to a place where drinking truth gets very personal—and perhaps even uncomfortable. Quite naturally, we tend to equate our purpose with visible success. In doing so, we seek to validate our existence *quantitatively*. How much money we give, how many committees we serve on, and how many people we help are all numerical measurements of what we have accomplished. Being spiritually fruitful is different because our influence cannot be measured. Those who seek purpose through success risk getting caught in a trap that hinders their ability to bear sweet spiritual fruit.

In the Western evangelical church, it is common to end a service with an altar call to give people the opportunity to receive Jesus Christ as their personal Savior. Recognizing that salvation comes through faith in Christ, people are encouraged simply to raise their hands—or to step forward to the front of the sanctuary—and repeat some form of what we call "the sinner's prayer." When a decision for Christ is made, the congregation celebrates, and the leaders make an effort to follow up with the new believer.

Through this simple methodology, millions of people have stepped into a relationship with God. But there is also a significant problem. Our evangelical altar call is a *cultural* practice that lacks the covenantal mindset of the Bible, and many people are ignorant of the depth of devotion that a covenant relationship demands. And though I am thankful for all who have come to Christ through crusade-style altar calls, I also think that we have lost a vital element of depth and devotion that is essential to Biblical Christianity.

Understanding what I do about covenants, I am inclined to think that a considerable number of people are Christians only in their minds. Individual judgment calls regarding salvation are not ours to make, but when little or no evidence of a changed life can be found, we have reason to be concerned. And the number of unchanged people who profess Christ is not small.

Furthermore, in our day, it is not uncommon for people to doubt their salvation. Even though they might have responded to an altar call, they remain uncertain of their spiritual status. But have you ever met a person who doubted whether he or she was married? Probably not. Why? Most marriages incorporate a covenant ceremony, which essentially seals the sanctity of the relationship. At the very least, they sign a legal document.

No doubt, the early church preached salvation by faith and not works, but other than the thief on the cross, you will be hard-pressed to find someone becoming a Christian without *immediately* being water baptized. Baptism was not an optional afterthought in New Testament times—it was integral to the salvation experience.

Can you imagine how committed people would be to God and His purposes if we required new Christians to participate in a blood covenant ceremony? Water baptism is no less sacred; it is the "covenant ceremony" by which we yield our entire being to God, bury our old self-oriented approach to life, and are raised by the power of God to a new life in Christ.

If a pastor announces that one hundred people made a decision for Christ, I might respond with a tepid clap. But if I hear about ten people getting baptized, my heart leaps with excitement! Baptism, by design, publicly proclaims our death to an old way of life and resurrection to a new existence in a covenant relationship with God.

I realize that immediate baptism is not always practical. I also understand that the Lord will meet us where we are and take whatever opportunity we give Him. At the same time, I think we can do much better than our often-revolving door of Christian involvement. The evangelical system is problematic when we present people with an opportunity to enter into a covenant relationship without at least challenging them to count the cost of a fully surrendered lifestyle.

When Jesus told His disciples, "This is the new covenant in My blood," He was initiating a brand new type of covenant relationship between God and humans, but one that followed the general pattern of His relationship with Abraham. Like Abraham, it is by faith that we enter into a covenant with God. If you are not in covenant with God, you are not a Christian. And if you have fully surrendered your life to enter into a sacred covenant with your Creator, why would you disobey the Biblical command by refusing to be water baptized?

COVENANT SALVATION

Many of our modern church problems are *systemic*. What I mean is that water baptism is not the primary issue. The bigger concern is that we have lost the covenantal mindset of the Scriptures and adopted a pragmatic approach to "get results." Altar calls yield numbers that a call for covenant baptism never will. Those numbers, in turn, can justify our ministries, pad our coffers, and bolster our egos. I am not saying that every pastor makes altar calls for selfish purposes, but that vain purposes have helped create an unhealthy system.

I understand the temptation that numbers present. When I present a report to our ministry board, I can easily quantify the number of books we distributed. Telling of transformed lives is much more difficult, if not impossible, since we never hear about much of what our ministry accomplishes. I understand, however, that God's definition of success differs vastly from ours, and so I make painstaking efforts to bear sweet and abundant fruit instead of getting caught up in a "numbers game." Thankfully, the Lord has given us ministry leaders and financial partners who understand these concepts.

Am I saying that numbers are unimportant? No. But numerical success can be both intoxicating and deceptive. More than once, I have dealt with a "successful" leader whose spiritual life was a sham. Naturally gifted leaders can move people to act, but it takes humble disciples of Jesus to grow people to maturity. In the natural world, reproduction is the product of maturity, and spiritual health follows suit to a degree. Numerical growth should flow from spiritual health.

When people make decisions for Christ, they enter into a sacred covenant with God and declare Jesus to be their *first love*. But what happens if, out of ignorance or willful neglect, they do not treat that relationship with the utmost importance? What if their experience is merely emotional, or if they view salvation as a consumer experience rather than the gateway to a devoted relationship with God? What if they seek to be blessed without becoming a blessing to others?

Time and space do not permit a historical review of the altar call's evolution, but I think we can learn something from one of the famed evangelists who helped make it popular—D. L. Moody. When people expressed an interest in salvation at Moody's meetings, he had them speak with laypeople trained as counselors for that meeting. This approach helped ensure that they understood what becoming a Christian involved. It also gave laypeople the opportunity to experience the joy of leading others into the salvation experience.

PURPOSE BEYOND OURSELVES

In essence, there can be no such thing as "consumer Christianity." The Lord created Eden as a free paradise with only one restrictive boundary: Do not eat from the tree of the knowledge of good and evil. He gave Adam and Eve the freedom to choose between life and death because love is always at the core of all God does.

The seeds of the forbidden fruit instilled a pervasive self-centeredness into the human heart. This self-centered focus has, in turn, corrupted and damaged relationships throughout history. But the Lord has always intended to bring us back. Even the Mosaic law, with its many rules and regulations, was rooted in love (Deuteronomy 30:6–14). In fact, all that was written in the pages of the Old Testament can be funneled into a love theme:

> One of them, a lawyer, asked Him a question, testing Him, "Teacher, which is the great commandment in the Law?" And He said to him, "'You shall love the Lord your God with all your heart, and with all your soul, and with all your mind.' This is the great and foremost commandment. The second is like it, 'You shall love your neighbor as yourself.' On these two commandments depend the whole Law and the Prophets."
> Matthew 22:35–40

Think about this passage for a second. Through the seemingly strange rules and sometimes sordid stories of the Old Testament, the Lord was mysteriously charting a course to bring humanity back to paradise. The essence of that paradise is found within the basic elements of faithfulness and love that characterize God's covenants. These covenant elements of faith and love, combined with God's blessing given to our forefather Abraham, again point us toward a purpose beyond ourselves. "And in you all the families of the earth will be blessed" (Genesis 12:3b).

Imagine yourself sitting in the royal palace of heaven. As you sit and relish the experience, a thousand thoughts flow through your mind. "This place is amazing! God is beyond description! With all the times I sinned against Him, I can hardly believe that I am here. I am so grateful that the Father sent Jesus to die for my sins and that Jesus lowered Himself to make such an extreme sacrifice." As you continue to soak in the moment, words of gratitude begin to flow from your lips, "Lord, thank You so much for all You have done to get me here. Is there any kindness that I can show You in return?"

Such a scenario is plausible. But there is also a problem. Our future place in heaven will do nothing to influence the current state of our world, and in this season, that is where our Lord's passions lie. We do not want to wait to express our covenant kindness to God. *Seeking to touch lives to bless our Savior is today's reality.*

Before he became king, David spent several years on the run, fleeing from King Saul's murderous efforts. During this season of his life, brave men began to gather around David. One particular event during that time fits our current discussion well:

> David had a craving and said, "Oh that someone would give me water to drink from the well of Bethlehem which is by the gate!" So the three mighty men broke through the camp of the Philistines, and drew water from the well of Bethlehem which was by the gate, and took it and brought it to David.
> 2 Samuel 23:15–16a

David's men felt so much loyalty and love toward their leader that they risked their lives to satisfy a mere craving. How much more should God's covenant children seek to fulfill the desires of their heavenly Father? And what does He desire? *The Lord wants to use us—as a unified body—to bless all the families of the earth.*

Being blessed by God means being used by Him to bless others, to live with a love-motivated purpose beyond ourselves. It does not matter whether we feel adequate or equipped—the Lord can deal with those issues just as He did with Moses—but that we live with the Lord's passions in mind. God's good plan for each of our lives will never be realized apart from our love-motivated service to others. Without being a blessing, we cannot be fully blessed.

OUR STEWARDSHIP

When a person takes a job, he or she is given a *sphere of influence* to manage. In essence, the person becomes a *steward* of that sphere, acting on behalf of the company to fulfill its purposes. A salesperson, for example, might cover a particular territory to make contacts and build relationships—all to sell a product to produce revenue. In our world's system, everything revolves around money.

A similar principle of stewardship applies to us as Christians—except our motivations are quite different. Each of us, whether great or small, has a *sphere of influence* in this world. That sphere will change with the seasons of our lives, but we never grow beyond the call to influence others for the glory of God.

The type of influence I am referring to is not political. Instead, through love, kindness, and good works, the Lord calls us to be witnesses of His goodness and His kingdom. Furthermore, participation in that kingdom is voluntary, so while we seek to persuade, we do not control or manipulate.

Our witness—the ability to influence others for eternal purposes—is one of the most precious and valuable gifts that God has given us. And as we learn and grow in the grace of God, so does our ability to influence others. One of the reasons that we live honest and just lives of integrity is to protect that witness. We lose credibility, and thus the ability to positively influence others for eternity, when our profession of faith in Christ conflicts with our lifestyle.

What if you have failed miserably or have been subject to a horrific past? The Lord will redeem and use those things too! *Our Creator is able to use every aspect of our lives for glorious purposes—if only we will believe and obey.* Each of us is unique. Family (or lack thereof), life experiences, personality, abilities, connections—all join to create a unique combination appropriate to our sphere.

LIVING OUT THE NEW COVENANT

I became a Christian while in college. My immediate sphere included my classmates and professors, as well as family members, friends, and neighbors from back home. After graduating, I began working in a laboratory and moved into an apartment. Debi and I then got married and joined a local church. Later, I switched jobs, and we brought children into this world. Each time, our sphere of influence changed. Sometimes it ebbed, and sometimes it grew, but the overall result was increase.

While serving on our church board, I also began to teach adult Sunday School classes, and it was there that my teaching gift began to emerge. The development of that gift further helped increase my sphere. Later, when an opportunity arose, Debi and I began to lead our church's college ministry. Soon I was teaching Bible studies, preaching for large group meetings, and speaking at conferences. With each season, I worked hard, developed my abilities, and built relationships. And with each season, my sphere grew.

Our college ministry efforts had matured significantly, but we felt we were called to an even broader sphere of influence. So, like a professional sports team trading away its high profile players for the sake of future potential, we surrendered much of that sphere to retool and rebuild. Starting all over again, we left college ministry and launched Search for Me Ministries to develop and distribute teaching materials.

It is difficult to capture the depth of our experience through a short summary, but through it all, Debi and I have sought to steward the calling and gifts that God has given us. We have sought to be faithful to His call regardless of our lot in life and how successful—or unsuccessful—our efforts appear to be. This desire to honor our Lord has led to long hours and lonely work when no one but God was watching. It has also meant considerable sacrifice—one of the key elements in our covenant stewardship.

I share a little of our ministry history to help you better understand the nature of new covenant living. God's stewards are not just those in "full-time" ministry. No matter your vocation or season in life, the Lord has a sphere for you to influence by word, by deed, by generosity, and by prayer. Are you being faithful to steward your witness and to fulfill His purposes for your life?

A LIVING SACRIFICE

Chapter twelve of Romans begins with Paul exhorting his readers to present themselves as "living sacrifices" for God:

> Therefore I urge you, brethren, by the mercies of God, to present your bodies a living and holy sacrifice, acceptable to God, which is your spiritual service of worship. Romans 12:1

As much as it goes against our natural preferences, there is a cost to being a faithful steward, but it is not as steep as we sometimes think.

When we make a divine exchange with God, we no doubt get the better end of the deal. The Lord takes our sin and our brokenness—even the curse that plagues our lives. In exchange, we receive forgiveness of all our sins, the indwelling presence of the Holy Spirit, new identities as children of God, and an eternal inheritance through becoming joint-heirs with Christ, among other things.

In a spiritual sense, this exchange with God resembles a financial transaction. Jesus paid a steep price to redeem us from slavery to sin, and our lives now belong to Him. This theme, the apostle Paul emphasizes well:

> Or do you not know that your body is a temple of the Holy Spirit who is in you, whom you have from God, and that you are not your own? For you have been bought with a price: therefore glorify God in your body. 1 Corinthians 6:19–20

> I have been crucified with Christ; and it is no longer I who live, but Christ lives in me; and the life which I now live in the flesh I live by faith in the Son of God, who loved me and gave Himself up for me. Galatians 2:20

Galatians 2:20, in particular, echoes a covenantal mindset. Jesus took our curse, punishment, and death, and our lives now belong to Him. Thus, we are no longer owners, but stewards of our own existence. Our hopes, our dreams, our finances, our families, and even our bodies belong to God.

Once, when a crowd of people began to gather around Jesus, He proclaimed that they had to carry their own crosses if they wanted to become His disciples (Luke 14:25–35). At this time, the Son of God also called people to "count the cost" of discipleship and surrender all their possessions. That sounds like covenantal language to me. And as ironic as it might sound, a life fully surrendered to God provides the best possible potential for being whole, blessed, and free.

It is with such a stewardship mentality that we become living sacrifices, governed by the *royal law* of love and liberty. In our God-given freedom, love binds us to God's purposes, and God's purposes center on the redemption and restoration of human lives. Jesus sacrificed that we might live, and we sacrifice that others might live. Such is the mindset of a covenant-friend of Jesus.

Living as a steward brings us back to a sense of purpose. We live with a purpose that transcends our own—a cause so profound that it stretches the limits of our imagination. Not by following rules and rituals, but by trusting and loving God, we have the opportunity to bring eternal blessings to others. Your faithfulness to fulfill His purposes, in other words, can mean life for a desperate soul.

EMPOWERMENT

If the idea of living as a steward for God's purposes sounds daunting, that is only because it is. How can ordinary, imperfect people be expected to live so selflessly, let alone fulfill a purpose beyond their natural abilities? The key lies in understanding the difference between a life of law and a life of grace.

Law burdens our shoulders with responsibilities, but provides no ability to fulfill them. On the contrary, when the Lord calls us to do something, He always provides us with what we need. He might not give us all that we want or all that we *think* we need, but where God calls, God provides.

Like Abraham, we are called to leave our comfort zones and take the apparent risk of venturing into the unknown in obedience to the Lord. Every time God commanded Abraham to do something, the man willingly obeyed, knowing that He would provide all that was needed. Professing Christians who refuse to step out in obedience to the Lord do not truly understand the essence of *faith expressing itself through love.*

Love is an action and not a feeling. For those who genuinely believe in the Lord, good works will follow. Faith produces love, and love leads to good, life-giving works in obedience to the Holy Spirit's leading.

> For by grace you have been saved through faith; and that not of yourselves, it is the gift of God; not as a result of works, so that no one may boast. For we are His workmanship, created in Christ Jesus for good works, which God prepared beforehand so that we would walk in them. Ephesians 2:8–10

In some religious circles, grace is almost nonexistent; people operate by a "salvation by works" mentality. By doing more good than bad, they believe they can earn entry through heaven's gates. But those who seek God's favor by being "good" people (i.e., using good works as a means of self-justification) are living out of the tree of the knowledge of good and evil. This means that they are enemies of God, seeking to usurp His royal throne. We can do nothing to "earn" our way into heaven; we can only respond with faith to what Jesus has already done.

On the opposite end of the spectrum are those who live with a one-dimensional understanding of God's grace. Grace, as taught by many in the church, is defined as "God's unmerited favor"—the means by which we are forgiven of our sins so that we can go to heaven. And while this definition of grace is entirely true, it also limits the greater emphasis of Scripture.

The concept of "passive grace" was foreign to the writers of the New Testament who understood that the baptism ceremony reflected an attitude of being "all in" for God. Faith and love, in a new covenant context, are active and not passive. Thus, we find in the book of Hebrews both a message of security for God's covenant children and dire warnings for those who fail to actively honor the sacred bond between God and humanity.

Romans, the book that lays out the New Testament gospel of grace better than any other, begins and ends with the idea that true faith leads us to obey God's commandments as we live out the essence of a covenant relationship.

> ... through whom we have received grace and apostleship to bring about the obedience of faith among all the Gentiles for His name's sake ... Romans 1:5

> ... but now is manifested, and by the Scriptures of the prophets, according to the commandment of the eternal God, has been made known to all the nations, leading to obedience of faith ... Romans 16:26

God's grace is multi-dimensional. Not only are we favored through the sacrificial work of Christ on the cross, the Holy Spirit of grace also empowers us to obey and serve the Lord's purposes. Grace, according to the greatest theologian among the apostles, is the mysterious power that enables us to labor and do good works for God:

> But by the grace of God I am what I am, and His grace toward me did not prove vain; but I labored even more than all of them, yet not I, but the grace of God with me. 1 Corinthians 15:10

Faith expressing itself through love. When we learn to move beyond obligation and live out of the simplicity of the gospel, the Holy Spirit of grace provides us with the ability to do *all* that God calls us to do.

A person who grasps the beauty and depths of God's grace will not sit idly by while the world sinks into death and despair. Instead, he or she will find both the power and desire to touch others with the heart of God's love. Such good works happen not by demand or obligation, but by the compelling power of love freely given.

Our motivation for serving and doing good works marks the difference between spiritual life and spiritual death. *We either serve because we love God and others, or because we love ourselves and view good works as a way to find divine favor.* A love motivation releases life and breeds good fruit, while selfishness makes us spiritually unfruitful—a state that is synonymous with being cursed. The concept is profoundly simple and yet amazingly powerful.

No matter how much we mature, our right standing with God comes through Christ and Christ alone. And yet, the extreme nature of His sacrifice calls for a wholehearted response. If we fail to respond by fully yielding our lives to God, we must question whether our belief possesses the substance of real faith or if it is merely wishful thinking.

COURAGE

As we bring this chapter to a close, we want to remember the wisdom of C. S. Lewis: "Courage is not simply one of the virtues, but the form of every virtue at the testing point." Whether you see yourself following in the footsteps of Jesus, Abraham, or some other spiritual great, you will need the fortitude to live contrary to human desires—your own included. The great heroes of the faith faced daunting circumstances, and yet they continued to trust and obey the heavenly Father. Today, we are blessed because those before us lived bravely.

When we enter into a new covenant relationship with God, we receive eternal spiritual blessings that are almost beyond our ability to grasp. But we also begin to find ourselves out of step with the worldly culture around us. To obey God rather than cower to the demands of human culture means that we must live bravely as well. As covenant children of God, we will need the courage to:

- Be different
- Be misunderstood
- Be criticized
- Offend people (without being offensive)
- Suffer public ridicule
- Suffer financial loss
- Lose vocational status
- Be rejected by family members
- Suffer physical harm

I am not saying that we will experience everything in the list above, but that all are possibilities. And regardless of the losses we suffer, our God will be faithful to keep us every step of the way.

We will all have times when circumstances make us think that God is unfaithful, but it is during these seasons that we must latch on and hold dearly to our Lord's covenant promises. Even the great heroes of the faith endured seasons when their circumstances made no apparent sense. That is why they are considered heroes of the faith. They trusted God when all natural appearances said otherwise.

Abraham and Sarah childless. Moses camping between the Egyptian army and the Red Sea. David fleeing from Saul. Daniel in exile in Babylon. Jesus hanging on the cross. And yet, unseen by natural eyes, God was working powerfully in each of these circumstances, His promises never wavering.

The day will come soon enough when the last taste of the Adamic curse is washed away, as we depart from this earth to be resurrected with new, sin-free bodies into eternal glory. On that day, we will see our Savior face to face, and we will understand that the covenantal mindset of the Bible was mercifully given to help us draw closer to our Creator. Until then, may we have the courage to hold on to His promises and live for His purposes. Surely, His faithfulness and lovingkindness extend to the heavens!

WRAP-UP

Is a covenant with the King of kings and Lord of lords worth the cost? That is a question that every person who encounters the gospel must answer. Drinking truth is not for the shallow soul. Ours is a chaotic world, driven by human demands and demonic agendas. To live out a covenant relationship with God, we will often find ourselves living out of step with the world around us—and even out of step with our own desires. But our lives are not our own; they belong to the Lord. He will use us in amazing ways if only we can gather the courage to live by a *faith expressing itself through love* mentality.

Adam's curse, which has dogged humanity since that fateful day in Eden, has been broken! As we live as faithful and fruitful stewards of God's goodness, we will both experience and share the rich blessings of Christ. Whatever God calls us to do, the Holy Spirit of grace will empower us to accomplish. Whatever we need, our covenant-Friend will provide. Then, after the smoke of this world clears, we will hear our Lord say, "Well done, good and faithful servant; enter into your rest." On that day, as we look at the many lives that our Savior has graced us to touch, we will say, "Wow! Look what the Lord has done!"

DISCUSSION

1. Why do we so often focus on being successful rather than fruitful?
2. What important purposes does water baptism serve?
3. Please read Matthew 22:35–40. What was Jesus communicating?
4. What does it mean to be a steward of God's purposes?
5. Talk about God's purposes for your life and how they relate to your current sphere of influence.
6. In what area of your life are you most in need of courage right now?

About the Author

Bob Santos writes to see lives transformed by God's goodness. Years of working in college ministry revealed that people crave to know more about God not only in their hearts through faith, but also through a deeper understanding of the truths found in His Word.

Pursuing spiritual vitality, Bob helps others "connect the dots" of Biblical truth by addressing "missing links" of contemporary theology. In this, Bob's books and video teachings explore key Biblical themes—such as covenants, grace, identity, rest, unity, and wisdom—that are often misunderstood or widely ignored. His explanations of difficult concepts, combined with inspirational messages of hope in Christ, are insightful, thought-provoking, and transformational as they explore the Christian faith in an understandable and yet intellectually satisfying way.

Bob was licensed for Christian ministry in 1997 and ordained in 2005 through Elim Fellowship (www.elimfellowship.org). In 2006, Bob and his wife Debi founded Search for Me Ministries, Inc. (sfme.org) with the mission to help form and equip a generation of world changers for Christ through the production of Biblically-based teaching resources.

College sweethearts, Bob and Debi have been married for over forty years. They have two adult children, two grandchildren, and three granddogs. When he is not writing, speaking, or leading a Bible study, you will likely find Bob doing something in the great outdoors.

Acknowledgments

SfMe Ministries is honored to serve the cause of Christ, but none of our work would be possible apart from those who serve, give, and pray for the sake of our ministry efforts.

A very special thank you goes to John Cavari, Bob Dunsmore, Paul Edwards, Howard Greenfield, Jason Hutchins, Lynda Logue, Crystal Min (crystalclearenglish.com), Samantha Mitchell, Todd Pugh, Elaine Rice, Rose Salazar, Debi Santos, Jodi Seidler, and John Stanko for their contributions to this book project. Thank you also to Katie Stevens for providing our internal artwork, Steve Margita for taking our cover photograph, K-Lee Gaffney for putting together the cover design, and Luke DeBuyser for being such an excellent hand model.

Additional Resources from Search for Me Ministries

Additional copies of **Drinking Truth** can be purchased through major online retailers. Volume discounts are also available for ministry organizations through SfMe Media (www.sfme.org). (Audiobook available)

Deciding what to teach and preach about can present a significant challenge for pastors and ministry leaders. *The Teleios Trail: Thirty Topics to Explore for Spiritual Growth* is an excellent resource to help grow spiritually mature disciples of Christ.

Division has long plagued the church, reflecting badly on Christianity and hindering our mission. *Greater Glory: The Transformational Power of Christian Unity* challenges us to embrace God's perspective so we can live out the lifestyle of love that is central to our faith. (Audiobook available)

There is a profound logic behind all that God does, but it is not human logic. *The Age of Abiding: Experiencing the Life of the Vine* provides powerful insights into human nature, helping the reader better grasp the mysterious beauty of the Christian gospel. (Audiobook available)

The Search for Rest: Fifty Days to a More Peaceful Life provides an awesome personal or group study that explores the concept of the Sabbath from both spiritual and physical perspectives. This thought-provoking book meets a powerful need in a world that is filled with anxiety and unrest. (Audiobook available)

The *Community Prayer Devotional* is a powerful book that brings churches together to pray. Even better, the cover can be personalized to fit your community, allowing people to take ownership and embrace prayer as a lifestyle! (Audiobook available)

If you want to gain a Biblical perspective on identity, *From Glory to Glory: Finding Real Significance in an Image-Driven World* is the book for you! Not only is this powerful forty-day devotional filled with illuminating insights, it will also help to renew your mind as a beloved child of the King of Glory. (Audiobook available)

Say Goodbye to Regret: Discovering the Secret to a Blessed Life is a life-changing book that deals with the problem of regret on two fronts. Learn how to move beyond the lingering pain of regret and also how to avoid regrets entirely by pursuing the rich treasures of God's spiritual wisdom. (Audiobook available)

The TouchPoint: Connecting with God through the Bible is a valuable resource for those who are interested in learning more about the Bible. Revised in 2020, this book provides a great introduction to the Christian Scriptures while emphasizing a personal relationship with God. (Audiobook available)

The Divine Progression of Grace: Blazing a Trail to Fruitful Living thoughtfully explores God's grace from a perspective of empowerment as well as acceptance. This book will take you deeper into a relationship with your Creator and also help make you more usable for His purposes.

Each reading in *Champions in the Wilderness: Fifty-Two Devotions to Guide and Strengthen Emerging Overcomers* draws from a deep well of truth to encourage, strengthen, and instruct those who desire to walk with God but are struggling in the face of adversity. The format of this devotional lends itself well to group discussion. (Audiobook available)

Posting Book Reviews

Please consider posting an online review of this book. Honest reviews are deeply appreciated and provide an easy way for our readers to contribute to our ministry efforts. Also, if your life has been touched by one of our resources, please recommend it to others.

SfMe Media

SfMe Media belongs to Search for Me Ministries, Inc. (SfMe Ministries)—an IRS-recognized 501(c)(3) nonprofit organization. Search for Me Ministries burns with a vision to help form and equip a generation of world changers for Christ. We believe in the importance of reaching those who do not know the Lord, but we also recognize the need for healthy churches as landing places for new believers. By helping Christians grow to maturity with our uniquely flavored teaching resources, we are helping to create environments that foster the fulfilment of the Great Commission in every way.

www.ingramcontent.com/pod-product-compliance
Lightning Source LLC
Chambersburg PA
CBHW052054110526
44591CB00013B/2203